What Every Middle School Teacher Should Know

What Every Middle School Teacher Should Know

TRUDY KNOWLES AND DAVE F. BROWN

NMSA

HEINEMANN
Portsmouth, NH

Heinemann
A division of Reed Elsevier Inc.
361 Hanover Street
Portsmouth, NH 03801-3912
www.heinemann.com

National Middle School Association
4151 Executive Parkway
Suite 300
Westerville, OH 43081
www.nmsa.org

Offices and agents throughout the world

The authors and publisher wish to thank those who have generously given permission to reprint borrowed material:

Excerpts from *Turning Points: Preparing American Youth for the 21st Century*, a report of the Carnegie Council on Adolescent Development. Copyright June 1989 by the Carnegie Council on Adolescent Development, a program of Carnegie Corporation of New York.

Library of Congress Cataloging-in-Publication Data
Knowles, Trudy.
    What every middle school teacher should know / Trudy Knowles and Dave F. Brown; [editor, Lois Bridges].
        p.   cm.
    Includes bibliographical references and index.
    ISBN 0-325-00266-5 (alk. paper)
    1. Middle school education—United States.   2. Adolescence—United States.   I. Brown, Dave F.   II. Bird, Lois Bridges.   III. Title.
LB1623.5 .K56 2000
373.236—dc21   00-039657

Editor: Lois Bridges
Production: Sonja Chapman
Cover design: Michael Leary
Manufacturing: Deanna Richardson

Printed in the United States of America on acid-free paper
04 03 02   RRD   5

Dedication

To Mom and Dad, who gave me life and taught me how to live it with abundant love.

T. K.

For my mother and father, whose confidence and support have opened so many doors, and for my daughters, Lindsay and Taylor, who bring me endless joy and gratification.

D. F. B.

Contents

Contents

Acknowledgments

This book grew out of our frustration at the lack of introductory books on middle level teaching that reflect the excitement and vibrancy of young adolescents. It took form with the help of numerous school systems, administrators, teachers, and particularly middle school students who have shared their ideas about what good middle level education is all about. It was completed with the guidance and support of friends, family, and colleagues. We would like to thank all those who helped this book become a reality.

About eight years ago, while teaching a class on middle level education at Todd County Middle School in Mission, South Dakota, I wrote a note to my coteacher, Cheryl Medearis, that read, "We should write a book." We never did, but Cheryl saved the note anyway. To Cheryl, thank you for your energy, dedication, beliefs, and mostly your laughter and friendship. To the teachers at Todd County Middle School, thank you for allowing Cheryl and me the freedom to experiment with ideas that became the foundation of this book.

I have had the pleasure of working with college students from two institutions. To my students at Sinte Gleska University in Mission, South Dakota, thank you for sharing your stories with me, for allowing me the freedom to formulate my philosophy, and for enriching my life. To my students at Westfield State College in Westfield, Massachusetts, thank you for your energy and for embracing middle level teaching so enthusiastically.

I believe strongly in the power of students to take control of their own learning. I want to thank the many great progressive educators who helped shape my philosophy about what good teaching is and can be. I want to particularly thank James Beane, who put a structure to my philosophy and who showed me what it means to continue to speak out, even in the face of overwhelming odds. I also want to thank all of the teachers I have met at the National Middle School Association (NMSA) who helped show me how that philosophy could be put into practice, in particular Barb and Carol.

Of course, this book would not have been possible without the help and support of many middle school teachers, administrators, and particularly students. They have taught me so much and strengthened my belief that we can always do better. Special thanks to all the middle school students who came to Westfield State to talk to future teachers. Their honesty and openness continue to be an inspiration to me. Thank you to Joann Tratiak, who believes so strongly in every student's right to be successful, and to her students in West Springfield, Massachusetts, who so graciously talked with me. A special thanks to the teachers and the students at Powder Mill Middle School in Southwick, Massachusetts, and to their principal, Pat Clem. They have so generously shared their expertise, time, stories, and lives with me and showed me what a great middle school can be.

Two middle school students deserve a special thanks: Eric Lund and Robert Smart. I know they will grow to be wonderful young men.

I am also grateful to those who contributed directly to this book. Richard Bordeaux allowed us to use his poetry, Scott Clark shared his thoughts on curriculum integration, and Lindsay Hamilton shared her drawing and poetry. A note of thanks also to the Carnegie Corporation, which so generously gave its permission to have portions of its report *Turning Points* reprinted in this book.

I would like to thank Anne Snell for reading and critiquing the manuscript. I am very grateful to her for her expertise and for being so supportive in everything I do. Gary Kime also gave feedback. I thank him for his insights and for a great night at Epcot. Lois Bridges has been an editor extraordinaire. I thank her most of all for believing in this project.

And there are the people whose emotional support made it possible to complete this task. To my family, especially Nancy, Anne, Rex, and Mark. Their love and support mean so much to me. To Mellissa, who has always encouraged me to follow my dreams and to jump even when it looked like I would fall. To Rachel, whose vision of the world is wonderful, and who has stood steadfast beside me and cried with me at Hallmark commercials. To Robert, who shared his stories, his energy, and his love, and has made life a true adventure. To Austin and Ariel, who have enriched my life in so many ways. To Dan, who has supported everything I've ever tried to do, including skydiving.

And to Dave, for helping my dream become a reality.

TRUDY KNOWLES

Trudy and I realized long ago that by listening to young adolescents and their teachers, the real stakeholders in the schooling process, we could discover the path to better teaching. Of course we realize that research in pedagogy is an integral part of how we can improve learning environments for young adolescents. But oh, what these middle school students have taught us these past five years!

Since 1995 Trudy and I have visited several middle schools and been granted access to interview teachers and students in many places. Quotations from teachers and students throughout the book were collected from interviews we conducted from 1995 through 1999. To those administrators who have paved the way, we are indebted to your contributions to this book. Among those providing their time and thoughts about middle level education were Ed Kershner, whose comments about the energy and enthusiasm of young adolescents are always enjoyed.

Several teachers were involved in interviews including the teachers at Valley Forge Middle School; teachers at Keith Valley Middle School; and several teachers at Conrad Weiser Middle School. Teachers and students both volunteered their time at Bala Cynwyd Middle School and Tilden Middle School. Three educators at Tilden have helped me to understand the role that they play in the lives of urban young adolescents, and I thank them for the ongoing discussion: Rodney Ash, Anita Nicholson, and principal, Nate Pettus. My discussions with Dave Flamer at the West Chester Area School District are encouraging as we work to move toward a true middle school model in its middle schools.

Acknowledgments

I thank Jerry Bellon for his advice about this project. Jerry has continued to provide guidance to me since I completed my doctoral program over ten years ago at the University of Tennessee. A special thanks to Gary Kime and a few colleagues of his at Radnor Middle School who provided feedback on the manuscript in its later stages. Tom Mastrilli from West Chester University was instrumental in helping us to format diagrams. I would like to thank Joe Varady for providing some exceptional and creative illustrations for the book. I would especially like to acknowledge the friendly cooperation from the administrators, teachers, parents, and students at Peirce Middle School.

Lois Bridges, our editor, is the world's best writing coach. Lois knows when to push, when to listen, and when to cheer. It has been a pleasure and an honor to work with such a fine professional. Her confidence in us is what took us over the top with this project.

Trudy had a vision of writing this book several years ago, and I'm thankful that she held on so tightly to it. The discussions, debates, arguments, and agreements about educational issues between Trudy and me are energizing. It's what being a professional educator is all about, and I am thankful that we have continued our professional relationship since graduating from the University of Tennessee.

I would like to especially recognize the support and companionship of Terry Rose. She has always been there for me and is a perfect model of effective teaching at the middle school and university levels.

My daughter, Lindsay, has listened intently to me as I have described the process of writing this book. I am thankful to Lindsay for her thoughtful words during this project.

DAVE F. BROWN

ONE

You Want to Be a What?

Middle School is very complicated.

ROBERT, AGE THIRTEEN

You are about to take a ride. Imagine that you are a new skier standing on the top of a mountain. You look down with fear. The only way to get to the bottom is to ski down, so you push your poles into the snow and begin. Suddenly you hit full speed. You are flying. You've never felt such exhilaration. Just as quickly, you lose control and fall down, not once, but again and again and again. You are ready to quit, but you are only halfway down the mountain, so you stand up one more time and promise

yourself that if you just make it down in one piece, you'll never attempt to ski again. You dig in your poles, take off, and soar to the bottom. Before you know it, you're on the ski lift again. You are halfway up the mountain before you realize you'll have to go down again. You know you'll fall, but you also know you'll fly. It's that one brief moment of flying that makes it all worthwhile.

The ride you are about to take is the ride of the middle school teacher. Going to school each day is exhilarating because you love your students. Sometimes you realize, however, that your emotional state matches that of your students, with all the ups and downs. You fall and get up again and again and again. At times you go home exhausted, wondering why you ever chose teaching as a career. The next day you're back in the classroom and you're soaring. You feel that you could teach forever. Teaching middle schoolers is not an easy trip, but the ride is exhilarating.

Who Are Young Adolescents?

What Are They Like?

What are they like, these young adolescents attending middle school? You've seen them. They're everywhere—walking in the mall, hanging out on street corners, living in your house. In fact, you were one, perhaps not so long ago. You know what they're like.

- They eat all the time.
- Their music is too loud.
- They take social issues very seriously.
- They frequently exclaim, "You don't understand."
- They cry a lot.
- They laugh a lot.
- They're sure that nobody has ever felt what they are feeling.
- They like hanging out at home and being with their parents.
- They hate hanging out at home or being seen with their parents.
- They have difficulty attending to something for more than a minute at a time.
- They are plagued with acne.
- They are seldom satisfied with the way they look.
- They're loyal to their friends.
- They talk behind their friends' backs.
- They outgrow their clothes every few months.
- Their voices crack when they sing in mixed chorus.
- They want to be independent.
- They don't want to let go of their childhood.

This time of vast emotional, social, physical, and cognitive change has been called pubescence, transescence, emergent adolescence, early adolescence, and young adolescence. Students at this stage are often called difficult, obnoxious, hard to handle, impossible, and hormonally driven. We would like to characterize this stage positively.

What should we call this time of change? *Transescence* is out. It is hard to say and sounds like a form of alien abduction. *Pubescence* suggests that the only significant aspect of this age is emerging sexuality. *Emergent adolescence* focuses too much on the future—on what will be instead of what is. What's left is *early* or *young adolescence*. Those are the terms we will use in this book.

How Do We Define Young Adolescence?

Should we define young adolescence according to age? Grade level? Physical attributes? Behaviors? Family or peer interactions? Emotions? Cognitive abilities? All of the above?

This period of time is characterized by vast developmental changes. Physical changes are more dramatic than at any other time in life except the fetal and early infancy stages. Cognitive changes create vast leaps in thinking ability. Social and emotional changes result in a move from dependence to independence. Some children begin these developmental changes at age ten, some not until fifteen. Most are somewhere in between. The definition of *young adolescence* is as complex as the people we are attempting to define.

Perhaps we don't need a definition. Perhaps, for purposes of this book, it is better to define early adolescence as the time a child spends in middle school. But that definition can also be complicated. Middle school grade configurations are not consistent. The most common grouping is sixth–eighth grade. You will also find middle schools that contain the fifth and/or ninth grade. And some only have seventh and eighth grade. Definitions, however, are not what the young adolescent is all about. Perhaps descriptions leading to understandings are a more appropriate way of explaining this age.

What Changes Occur During This Time?

The changes that young adolescents undergo are distinctive. Adolescence is not like any other time of life and no young adolescent is like any other.

Growth at this time is inconsistent from one individual to the next. Developmental stages are uneven and follow no set timeline. Middle school students can be physically mature young women, or girls who have not yet experienced their first menses; they might be fully grown young men, or boys barely five feet tall. Their social and emotional actions can range from childlike behaviors to adult perceptions. Take a look in the middle school cafeteria, and you'll see them all.

Other transformations are occurring. Young adolescents are transitioning from the dependence of childhood to the independence of adulthood. They are moving from the safety and security of their families to the insecurity of finding a place for themselves in the adult world.

Early adolescence is a time when children develop a sense of who they are independent of anyone else; when they learn to interact socially and act responsibly. It is a time when they develop their values and character, expand their interests, and pursue their dreams. If we want students to be successful in middle school, we must pay attention to the changes in their development, understand the challenges that lie ahead of them, and listen to what they say.

Becoming a Middle Level Teacher

Time for Reflection

Why do you or did you want to be a middle school teacher? What characteristics do you think a middle school teacher needs to have?

Middle Level Certification

Middle school teachers in the past often came from the ranks of elementary school faculty. Teachers would explain, "I really wanted to teach second grade but this was the only job I could get." Others came from the ranks of high school educators: "I really wanted to teach eleventh grade American history and government, but this was the only job I could get." In some states, certification still covers K–8 or

6–12. In many other states however specific training for middle level teachers is now required and for good reason. Although we have always been aware of the developmental issues of the early adolescent, calls for specially trained teachers have increased since the late 1980s when the Carnegie Council on Adolescent Development published its report *Turning Points* (1989). The authors of *Turning Points* focused on the vital importance of developing middle schools that are responsive to young adolescents' developmental needs. Such a process requires trained middle level teachers who have a thorough background in young adolescent development.

With new certification requirements, college and university education programs faced the challenge of restructuring teacher education programs to include a specific focus on middle level preparation. Despite the necessity for such a focus, the results of a survey conducted in five states that require middle grades certification indicated that less than one-fourth of the middle school teachers had participated in a specific program that prepared them to work with young adolescents (Scales and McEwin 1994).

Characteristics of Effective Middle Level Teachers

If you are in a middle level certification program or hold a middle level teaching certificate, consider yourself fortunate. Being enrolled in a specific middle grades certification program and getting your teaching certificate, however, is not enough. In addition, you will need several personal and professional characteristics that you demonstrate daily as a classroom teacher. How does your list of characteristics match ours?

As a middle level teacher you will need:

- a sense of humor that you share with students regularly
- flexibility that you demonstrate in your instructional and curricular planning and delivery
- the ability to actively listen to your students
- the ability to show unconditional caring for young adolescent students
- a contagious passion for learning

- a willingness to move beyond the boundaries of your subject area training
- a philosophy and action plan that places students at the center of the learning process
- a belief in the process of collaborating with students regarding instruction and curriculum
- the confidence to guide students on their path to learning
- an awareness of adolescent health issues, and a willingness to address these issues with students
- a strong sense of your own identity
- a wealth of knowledge about young adolescent development
- a belief in all students' ability to succeed
- knowledge and skills to help all students achieve success

Naturally, the list could go on. As you read through this book, ask yourself if you have the characteristics necessary to be an effective middle school teacher. You will also want to add to the list and begin piecing together the puzzle of what effective middle level teaching involves.

Time for Reflection

What questions or concerns do you have about young adolescents or the structure of the middle school?

What questions or concerns do you have about being a middle school teacher?

What do you think is the most important thing a middle school student can do or learn in school?

Your answers to the first two questions will become the basis for your inquiry into middle level education. Your answer to the third will develop into your philosophy of learning at the middle level. This book will enable you to explore your questions concerning middle level education. Chapter 2 focuses on the development of the young adolescent and builds a framework for a developmentally responsive middle school. Chapter 3 provides a historical overview of the middle school movement, while Chapter 4 explains how to develop communities of learning. From this initial framework, we provide the design of a middle school environment that is developmentally responsive to young adolescent needs and will help them move successfully toward becoming independent adults.

Chapters 5, 6, and 7 explore the important issues of curriculum, instruction, and assessment. Chapter 8 examines structural and organizational issues relevant to appropriate middle level education. We end with a discussion on how to be an advocate for middle level education and young adolescents, providing a way for you to reflect on your role as a middle level professional educator.

We hope that in this book, you will find the answers to many of your questions. We suspect that in your reading of it, you will generate additional questions. In fact, we hope this is the case. Learning begins with asking questions, and the most effective teachers are inspired by their own quest for learning.

So hold onto your hat. We believe working with young adolescents will be the most exhilarating ride you will ever take.

References

CARNEGIE COUNCIL ON ADOLESCENT DEVELOPMENT. 1989. *Turning Points: Preparing American Youth for the 21st Century*. New York: Carnegie Corporation.

SCALES, P. C., AND C. K. MCEWIN. 1994. *Growing Pains: The Making of America's Middle School Teachers*. Columbus, OH: National Middle School Association.

TWO

Understanding the Young Adolescent

Being a young adolescent is very cool because you're going through lots of changes—like, your body is changing and your voice is cracking and it's a new environment. And I'm meeting lots of people I never met before and switching class. I don't have recess anymore.

ERIC, AGE THIRTEEN

Early adolescence can be a tough time for children. Their bodies and minds are changing, creating a preoccupation with self-examination as they strive to discover and craft a personality. As the young adolescent begins to foster independence from the family, social interaction with peers becomes very important. It's not always easy to cope with such rapid and dramatic changes. One thirteen-year-old, Evan, described the difficulty he experienced: "It's a really tough time. You're not a teenager but you're not a baby. I think it would be easier if you were an adult or younger."

Creating a school environment that is responsive to the changing needs of young adolescents requires an understanding of their developmental changes. More importantly, however, it requires an understanding of how young adolescents perceive those changes. Their perceptions become their reality.

Here is how Lindsay, an eighth grade student, describes herself in both poetry and art.

What's on the Inside

I am an artist,
who draws what she feels, sees, and encounters,
I need love from my friends and family,
I need affection to help me be successful in life,
I want to be all I can be,
To do this I will work hard to achieve,
I am human,
I make mistakes and learn from them,
I will not give up and therefore,
I will be the best by being me.

LINDSAY HAMILTON

LOVE
FAITH
FRIENDS
FETISHES
DREAMS
CHERISH
HOPES
NEEDS
WANTS
FEELINGS
LIVES
ENCOUNTERS
WONDERS
FREEDOM
GROOVES
PEOPLE
NATURE
LIGHT
DARK
FLAVOR
INDEPENDENCE

Lindsay's self-description

What is happening to these young people? This chapter will explore the physical, cognitive, social, and emotional changes that occur in young adolescents, and pave the way for our discussion of a school environment that is responsive to these changes. By understanding their needs and listening to their perceptions, perhaps we can be more responsive to their reality.

Time for Reflection

Dig through some old pictures of yourself and find one from your middle school years. Write a few thoughts about how you felt about yourself during that time of your life.

Physical Development

The greatest problem for middle schoolers is growing up too fast.

BESSIE, AGE THIRTEEN

I've changed physically. I've gotten so out of shape. I come home so tired every day. All I want to do is eat. I gained twenty pounds this year.

DAN, AGE TWELVE

Photo day arrives at Smith Middle School. Students line up from shortest to tallest and march into the gym to have their pictures taken. There they stand: from four feet nine inches to six feet two inches. Six months ago, they were much more similar in size. What is happening to these kids?

It's puberty—a word that strikes fear in the hearts of parents and confusion in the hearts of the young adolescent. When does it start? When does it end? Does puberty start when the physical changes begin? For some that may be as early as ten or as late as fifteen. Does it start when the child goes to middle school? That may be fifth, sixth, or seventh grade. If we can't even define when it starts, how will we know how to address it?

Physical development is one of the overriding concerns of young adolescents. Looking at themselves in every mirror they can find, they will often see an alien body staring back. Whether it's in the bathroom mirror at home or the one hung in their locker, the reflection in the window of a car, the door knob to their classroom, or cafeteria spoon, middle school students watch themselves, convinced that everyone else is watching them too. They want to know, "Am I normal?"

A story a former school administrator tells emphasizes the need young adolescents have for self-examination (Blackburn 1999). A middle school principal was receiving complaints from teachers in the building that students were constantly asking for the restroom pass during class time. Annoyed by the students' need to leave the room during lessons, the teachers were looking for solutions. The perceptive principal asked the central office administrator to purchase mirrors for every classroom. The mirrors were placed strategically inside the door of each classroom. The result was an amazing drop in the number of student requests for restroom breaks.

Young adolescents' concerns about their bodies are manifested in social and emotional reactions that may affect their ability to learn. Our understanding of physical development is vital, therefore, if we want to create an environment conducive to learning. The rate of physical development in young adolescents may vary from one student to the next, but there are common mileposts.

Physical Changes

The Growth Spurt

Beginning at about age ten for girls and twelve for boys, individuals experience a growth spurt of the skeletal and muscular systems. The sequences of the changes tend to be somewhat consistent, although individual variations occur. What is less standardized is the age and speed at which the changes happen (Tanner 1972).

Height gain may be as much as four or more inches a year in young adolescents, with usually two years of fast growth followed by three years of slow steady growth. That could mean the addition of ten to twenty inches in just five years. Average height gain during adolescence for females is seven inches; for males, it is nine to ten inches.

Weight gains equal eight to ten pounds a year. Many young adolescents gain as much as forty to fifty pounds before it's all over. One middle schooler told us, "I gained ten pounds in six months. I'm not too proud of that." Another student added, "In the last year I've grown a lot—four or five inches."

Skeletal and Muscular Changes
A defining characteristic of the physical development of young adolescents is rapid and uneven skeletal change. The bones in the legs may grow when nothing else seems to be growing, giving young adolescents the appearance of being all legs. The feet may grow while height remains constant. Arms may lengthen while the torso stays the same. The hands may seem disproportionately large.

The result is "the awkward stage." In June of one year, the body is well proportioned; the student is an exceptional athlete. The following June, the child is lanky and graceless. What happened to the physical coordination of just a year before?

To complicate matters further, bone growth tends to surpass muscle growth (Tanner 1972). This variable development is significant particularly in physical education and sports programs, where kids are often encouraged to lift weights and throw curve balls when their muscles cannot sustain the effort.

Van Hoose and Strahan (1988) report that another result of the changing skeletal structure of young adolescents is that the three tailbones fuse and harden into their final adult form. It is a process that can cause pain and discomfort. Eric reports that, "Sometimes when the teachers are not looking, I need to stand." When Tom, age thirteen, was asked what we would change about school, he commented, "I would change the chairs. We have hard rock chairs and it hurts after awhile."

Long bones, awkwardness, underdeveloped muscles, pain in the tailbone, huge feet, long hands; no wonder the young adolescent is concerned. Despite these uncomfortable growing pains, we put them in a school setting where they have to sit for most of the day.

Hormones

> I know everything I need to know about being an adolescent. You
> grow hair on your chin and want to have sex all the time.
>
> ROBERT, AGE TEN

Hormones have gotten a bad rap in discussions about young adolescents; they are often blamed for behaviors that many adults don't seem to understand. It is true that hormones play a powerful role in development. If we understand their role, we can better understand young adolescent behaviors.

The body prepares for full sexual maturity during early adolescence, resulting in reproductive capability. Males and females experience increases in the amount of the hormones testosterone and estradiol during puberty that affect sexual development. The most dramatic increase for males is in testosterone—levels of this hormone are sometimes eighteen times what they were before puberty. The primary increase for females is in the hormone estradiol—levels are approximately eight times what they were before puberty (Nottelmann et al. 1987). During early adolescence, these hormonal changes result in the development of primary and secondary sex characteristics.

Primary characteristics are those changes that occur in preparing the body for full reproductive capability. In females, the major benchmark is menstruation—accompanied by the fear in girls that they'll be the last in their peer group to experience it. The primary characteristic for males is testicle and penile growth. Finally, males experience that first ejaculation, alone, at night, under the covers: fully experienced, rarely discussed.

Secondary characteristics include physical changes not necessarily related to reproduction. Secondary sex characteristics for females include breast development—often accompanied by behavioral changes such as the wearing of baggy shirts, the adoption of an erect, proud walk, or a slumping of the shoulders in an effort to conceal development; the growth of pubic and underarm hair; and rounding of the hips. Changes for males include facial, underarm, and pubic hair growth, and the ever embarrassing lowering of the voice.

Changes in reproductive maturity are beginning earlier than in past generations. For example, in the United States in 1900 the average age of a female's first menstruation was just over fourteen years. The average age today is slightly over twelve (Santrock and Yussen 1992). Earlier development results in physically mature boys and girls without the cognitive and emotional maturity necessary to understand those changes.

The sex hormones are not the only hormones undergoing changes. Hormonal secretions dictated by the pituitary gland also increase, often in an irregular way. For example, sudden secretions of adrenaline into the body from the adrenal gland could make the young adolescent want to run around the school building ten times just when asked to sit and do a worksheet. At other times the gland is underactive, resulting in lethargy (Van Hoose and Strahan 1988). Peter, a sixth grader, describes the result of these physical changes; "One of the hardest things for me is just waking up in the morning and going through the day without pulses of tiredness. Sometimes I get real restless because I get really tired."

Sweat glands also become very active, explaining why classroom windows are frequently open even in the dead of winter. Active sweat glands also contribute to oily hair and the development of that scourge of adolescent—acne.

The Appetite—Insatiable and Peculiar

Young adolescents have high nutrient requirements due to the rapid growth of the skeletal system and other physical changes. It is not uncommon for a young adolescent to eat continuously from the time they get home from school until bedtime. Unfortunately, due to the cultural prevalence of fast food, many of these kids are not eating foods that give them the maximum benefit. In addition, in schools that serve lunch at 10:30, students may not be getting the appropriate nutrition they need for effective learning later in the day.

Developmental Variations

Gender Distinctions

Girls' growth spurts peak about two years earlier than boys' (average age twelve for girls, compared with fourteen for boys). Attend a middle school dance, and you will observe this phenomenon firsthand: five-foot-five-inch girls dancing with five-foot-one-inch boys. Suddenly girls are taller, stronger, and more mature than boys.

Middle school girls seem to struggle more with their physical changes and tend to be more concerned with physical appearance. The result is a lowering of self-esteem as well as an increase in self-consciousness (Simmons and Blyth 1987). This concern undoubtedly has something to do with gender stereotypes, put forward by the media, dictating that females should be attractive while boys should be rugged. Media images remain a powerful force. Rarely do adult perspectives have the kind of influence that peer opinions and advertising campaigns have on young adolescent minds.

Individual Differences

Young adolescent development does not follow a strict timeline. Individual differences occur both between and within each gender. Everyone is developing at a different rate and yet everyone is on track. These variations make it difficult for young adolescents to find someone with whom to compare their bodies. How do they know if they are all right—if they are "normal"? Joel Milgram (1992) explains: "The pace of the physical changes taking place is different for each child and for each sex. In the egocentric, comparative world of the young adolescent, these differences are generally translated into feelings of inadequacy and deficiency. . . . It is important to remember that all adolescents at one time or another feel badly about some part of their bodies" (19).

Not surprisingly, talking about the physical changes seems to be more difficult for the young adolescent than talking about newfound friends, mood swings, or what they'd like to see their teachers do in the classroom. The physical changes have such a dramatic impact on emotions, learning, and social interactions that discussing them can make perceived inadequacies seem even more real. Think back on your own early adolescence. How willing were you and your friends to discuss breast development, underarm hair, wet dreams, or vocal changes? Instead, less emotionally charged issues like shoe size tend to be discussed instead of the more serious topics that affect an individual's sense of self.

15

Impact of Physical Changes

The middle school years are a time of personal criticism. Due to the young adolescent's ever increasing self-awareness, the timing of certain physical changes can and does heavily impact self-consciousness. Young adolescents can be found carefully examining themselves as their curiosity becomes aroused by these physical changes.

Ask seven-year-olds about the growth of their bodies and typically they'll express disinterest. Four years later the young adolescent is obsessed by these physical transformations. Few adults have positive memories about the way they looked during young adolescence. M. R. Wright, in a 1989 study of body image in adolescence, commented, "Preoccupation with one's body image is strong throughout adolescence, but it is especially acute during puberty, a time when adolescents are more dissatisfied with their bodies than in late adolescence."

Debate continues over whether early or late maturers experience more difficulties. In her study of 335 adolescents over a three-year period from sixth through eighth grade and during their last year of high school, Petersen (1987) found that late or early maturation affected individual satisfaction with appearance. She reported that studies conducted in the 1960s found that early-maturing males were more successful at peer relations during middle and high school. These individuals excelled in athletics, demonstrated confidence in social situations, and became the school leaders. The studies showed, furthermore, that when the late-maturing boys reached their thirties, they had a stronger sense of identity. Girls in the seventh and eighth grades seemed less satisfied if they were early maturers. Although these girls were seen as more popular, at a personal level they were often self-conscious and insecure. Petersen's study also showed that early maturers tended to get higher grades. Could this be due to teachers' perceptions of performance based on physical development?

But dealing with the young adolescent's self-image is not simply a matter of identifying whether a child is an early or late maturer. As Tanner (1972) reports, "There is little doubt that being an early or late maturer may have repercussions on behavior, and that in some children these repercussions may be considerable" (19). Teachers must be aware of the facts of development and be ready and willing to discuss developmental issues with their students and, perhaps, with students' parents. Students must be made aware that they are developing normally, whatever their rate or sequence of physical maturation.

Physical development is only one aspect to consider when looking at the young adolescent. Although physical changes are the most obvious and visible of the changes, it is the impact of physical maturation on emotional and social development that has the greatest influence on how young adolescents view themselves, school life, and those around them.

Intellectual Development

Early adolescence is a time when intellectual functioning frequently changes due to brain growth and increasing neural connections as well as an expanding social world. Young adolescents tend to be intensely curious; they also display a wide range of skills and abilities. Just what are they thinking?

Piaget's Findings

Jean Piaget (1977a) provides us with perhaps the clearest picture of what may be happening cognitively and intellectually to the young adolescent. Piaget developed a theory about how people make sense of their world. In this process, he identified four stages of intellectual development. Each of the stages reflects characteristics related to a person's cognitive ability with respect to object perception. The stages are: sensorimotor (birth to two years), preoperational (two to seven years), concrete operational (seven to eleven years) and formal operational (twelve years to adulthood). Individuals pass through each stage in sequence, but at varying rates.

With the young adolescent we are most concerned with the stages of concrete and formal operations. In the concrete stage, students can classify and order objects, reverse processes, think of more than one thing at a time, and think logically about concrete objects. They still need direct experiences and do better with real as opposed to abstract objects or thought. Middle level students in this concrete state of cognitive growth are better able to cognitively grasp abstract principles when ideas are taught with the use of hands-on activities and materials rather than presented in a lecture or by reading a textbook. Middle level teachers should stock their classrooms with many genuine objects (manipulatives) that help students to actually touch and see the concepts that they are learning. Although manipulatives, role-playing and hands-on activities are important during all stages, they are particularly important during the concrete stage.

In the formal operational stage, students have developed the capability of solving abstract and hypothetical problems. According to Piaget (1977a), "This period is characterized in general by the conquest of a new mode of reasoning, one that is no longer limited exclusively to dealing with objects or directly representable realities, but also employs hypotheses" (33). Elements of formal thought include the following:

1.   An increased ability to think in hypothetical ways about abstract ideas as well as to generate and test hypotheses systematically. When asked how his thinking had changed, Rob (age fourteen) responded, "I think I examine problems more and try to put the problem with something else I already know."

2.   An ability to think about the future and, therefore, to plan and explore—hence middle school students' sudden preoccupation with life plans and their concern for the world around them.

3.   *Metacognition,* or the ability to reflect on one's thoughts. Caine and Caine (1994) describe metacognition as "thinking about the way we think, feel and act" (160). When a seventh grader doesn't understand something, he/she can suddenly think about not understanding. Such thinking may not lead to understanding and may in fact lead to frustration. Indeed, many of the frustrations middle school students experience may result from this new reflective thought—this thinking about thinking. They may even worry about why they are thinking about their thinking.

For the early adolescent, the growth of metacognitive abilities generates greater understanding of abstract principles and results in more meaningful learning. The development of these self-reflective processes may not always be focused on academics. Young adolescents simultaneously become focused on social concerns, physical growth changes, and emotional and moral issues.

4. Idealism, expanded possibilities, and expansion of thoughts. The middle school student's mind is suddenly open to a myriad of ideas, solutions, and imaginings. The ability to think hypothetically produces unconstrained thoughts and a sense of unlimited possibilities. "Reality" is no longer the benchmark of thought, having been overtaken instead by "what is possible."

Moving from Concrete to Formal Thought Processes

Implications for Instruction

In studying Piaget's theory, we can assume that most students will be in the concrete operational stage as they enter middle school and experience periods of formal operational thought by the time they leave. Middle school then becomes a period of cognitive transition. Although this idea sounds good in theory, many students remain primarily in the concrete operations stage of development throughout their middle school careers, with only about one-third of eighth graders consistently demonstrating an ability to use formal operations (Piaget 1977b). Lounsbury and Clark (1990) indicate that academically talented eighth graders often experience confusion because they are in the process of adjusting to and accommodating more powerful cognitive strategies. An eighth-grade teacher describes the frustration in teaching young adolescents: "I think my biggest challenge is getting all the kids in the class to reach the same conclusions and the same level of thinking—which I can't do. So, when I have a question as to why something happens, I have some kids who are wondering what's happened."

Variations among students are common. So are variations in individuals with respect to different subject areas. The young adolescent may be capable of abstract thinking in mathematics yet not be able to set up a scientific experiment. Students at this stage move back and forth between concrete and formal operational thought. These variations have great implications for instruction, as Van Hoose and Strahan (1988) noted: "Planning instruction is like shooting at a moving target due to rapid, individual changes" (16).

Egocentrism

One aspect of young adolescents' thinking is a new form of egocentrism. Unlike the egocentrism of younger children, who assume that others think the same way they do about everything, young adolescents begin to understand that people have different beliefs and attitudes. They become immersed in their own thinking. They reflect on and analyze their thoughts and assume that everyone is as interested in their ideas as they are. A typical thought process is, "Because I am thinking about me, then everyone must be thinking about me. Because I notice my hair, everyone else must be looking at it. Since I pay attention to myself, everyone else must be paying attention to me."

Another result of expanding thought processes is the sense of personal uniqueness and infallibility. Middle school students are certain that no one has ever thought the thoughts they are thinking or felt the feelings they are feeling. As they get caught up in their personal worlds, young adolescents can become removed from reality and begin to feel indestructible. The belief that "it won't happen to me" contributes to risk-taking behaviors.

When students are given opportunities to test out possibilities and try out new ideas during the middle school years, they become less egocentric and more realistic. During middle and late adolescence, a more balanced perspective is usually achieved.

The Curiosity Factor

Middle school students are learners in the purest sense of the word. Based on a developing capacity for abstract thinking, middle school students are curious about life and highly inquisitive about everything life has to offer. They challenge principles that don't fit their view of the way things work. This curiosity leads to the desire to participate in practical problem solving and activities that reflect real issues.

The curiosity factor is reflected clearly in the following poem written by a college student reflecting on his middle school years.

I Wanna Know

I wanna know
How trees are made
And why money's paid

I wanna know
How stars are so bright
And why lights light

I wanna know
How animals mate
And why people hate.

I wanna know
How pollution starts
And why mountains fall apart.

I wanna know
How people breathe
And why birds fly with ease.

I wanna know!

RICHARD BORDEAUX

The bodies of young adolescents are physically maturing; their minds are thinking in ways that they have never been able to think before. Both of those developmental changes affect social interactions and impact the young adolescent's emotional life.

Social Development

At a time when dramatic physical and intellectual changes are occurring, children are taken from the safety and security of the self-contained elementary school and put in an alien environment. They often go to larger schools that include students they've never met before. They change classes and are responsible for being at certain places at certain times. As frightening as this new setting appears, it also provides the exciting and challenging prospect of meeting new people and gaining increased control of their lives. Bordeaux (1993) reflects on this prospect in the following poem.

Finding a Place In the Group
Alone
In the back of the room
with this growing sense of doom
Laughter to the left of me
Smiling to the right.
Alone in the middle
No land in sight
Drowning in fright
Hey, somebody
Anybody
throw me a line
and I'll be fine
I'll pull myself in
Show you what's within
Give you the straight poop
And maybe
Just maybe
Find my place in the group.

Sheila, a seventh grader, was asked what she liked best about middle school. She responded, "Coming and seeing my friends and stuff." When asked what was the most important thing to learn in school Peter responded, "How to make friends and how to act. Some people are just naturally more popular than others and they make friends more easily for some reason. But I think if you're not one of those people you have to learn the harder way—worrying about if people like you, or hate you, or whatever." Eric, also a seventh grader, agreed. "Social abilities are the most important thing to do and learn—getting in touch with the world and knowing what's going on and being able to talk in front of people."

Their teachers agree. When asked about the most important thing a middle school student should do or learn in school their responses are surprisingly similar: "How to get along"; "Social interactions along with social responsibility"; "Socialization"; "Social interaction with fellow peers and adults." Although academics remain important in preparing these students for life, teachers acknowledge the vital role that socialization plays during the middle school years. The tremendous social needs of the middle school student should be taken into account in designing the structure, curriculum, and instruction of middle schools.

The Role of the Family

In their attempt to move from dependence to independence, the social affiliations of the young adolescent broaden, with allegiance split between the family and the peer group. Although authority remains primarily with the family, young adolescents want to begin making their own choices about what to do and who to do it with. Never before has the child had an opportunity to make the kinds of choices that are being offered in middle school.

Parents begin to lose their omnipotence and are no longer infallible in the eyes of their child. Suddenly the parents don't know all the answers to the homework questions and their behaviors can be seen by the young adolescent as inappropriate. Parents are an embarrassment.

The early adolescent struggles with the conflict inherent in the need to depend on parents for support as they move toward independence. The seventh grader who occasionally asks her parents for assistance in doing homework may request that her father drop her off a block away from school to ensure that he not embarrass her in front of her friends. At the end of the day, when the father returns to the same intersection to pick his daughter up, she chastises him for not driving to the school building to retrieve her.

In order to conform to the desires of a new social group, early adolescents may appear to renounce any loyalty they previously had to parents. As peers gain importance, the young adolescent, in an attempt to try out new roles, may reject directions or suggestions from the family and challenge previously held beliefs that the parents had so carefully inculcated. Although other adults may continue to have a strong influence, the young adolescent desires and searches for increased decision-making opportunities. Parents become confused about whether to offer assistance or let the child alone.

Despite the young adolescent's apparent rejection of parental authority, parents continue to play a primary role in the young adolescent's life. When asked who the most important person was in their life, young adolescents we interviewed almost universally picked one or both of their parents:

> "I'd say my dad. He always helps me. He'll help me understand things better like in school."
> "My parents. They pretty much make you the person you are. If you're little, they guide you. They teach you your manners, they teach you what to do."
> "My parents. They teach me the important lessons."
> "My parents because I love them so much. They take good care of me and they're nice to me."
> "I think my parents. I have a really close relationship with them. I definitely think they help me a lot. I really look up to them."
> "My mother because two years ago my dad died, and my mother had to take over two parts of the family."
> "My parents because they kind of explain things to me."

Young adolescents need stability and security in a world that sometimes seems upside-down and is certainly confusing. Although parents may be equally confused, they can provide the stability and security that the child needs.

The Role of Peers

Making friends at the middle school level is probably one of the first true choices a child has the opportunity to make. The child doesn't get to choose his or her parents or where to go to school. During elementary school, friends were usually those who lived in your neighborhood or attended your elementary school. Prior to this time the only models of behavior were family members, teachers, adults in the community, and maybe sports or entertainment stars.

A whole new world opens up during middle school. This expanding social landscape creates questions in young adolescents' minds about how to get peers to like them. They begin to see that some kids are popular while others aren't. They wonder how that happens, and how they can become part of the popular group. They question where they stand and wonder how their peers think of them (Rice 1999).

The young adolescents' world has changed: new lifestyles, ways of thinking, values, and ideas are continually presented. The peer group is the primary source of new standards and models of behavior. Being part of the group helps young adolescents develop different points of view and try out new ideas. Experimenting with different ways of thinking and behaving is a vital component of the search for personal identity. Peers aid in this development by offering feedback on clothes, appearance, behavior, and anything else that interests them. The feedback allows young adolescents to gauge their new patterns of behavior in search for what fits.

The desire for peer approval is an extension of the desire to have their personal choices validated. The group also allows young adolescents to cover up what they believe are inadequacies. Since young adolescents no longer know what is normal, they lean heavily on peers to provide a structure for new behaviors and count on their peers to lead them in the right direction. This conformity to behavioral norms can have both positive and negative ramifications.

Initially in middle school, the need for companionship and social interaction leads students to develop same-sex friendships. Although interest in the opposite sex emerges, often in the form of what is called puppy love, same-sex affiliation continues to dominate and is preferred by the middle school student (Milgram 1992). Sex roles begin to change but it is often the parents, teachers, other adults, or the media that encourage that change and stress opposite-sex relationships. Informal and sometimes formal dances encourage young adolescents to form relationships at a time when they may prefer friendly interactions, long phone calls, mixed group activities, and casual flirting.

Peer pressure is real to the young adolescent. During this stage, as young adolescents try to fit in, they become impressionable to what other people have to say about them, particularly if it is negative. One student, when asked about peer pressure said, "You gotta fit in so you get good friends."

When asked what the greatest problem for middle school students is, Celeste, an eighth grader, responded, "Smoking, peer pressure, and trying to fit in." Her friend Melissa continued, "A few (students) got caught with marijuana; someone got suspended for carrying a pack of cigarettes; I also think graffiti—people draw on the walls. People were dyeing their hair with markers."

Why do they engage in such behaviors? To be accepted by a group. Parents may not approve, but middle schoolers are more encouraged by the approval of their peers than the disapproval of their parents. When asked what the biggest problem middle school students have to face, Eric, age thirteen, said, "Not getting along with kids. Having them tease you."

Although parents and teachers worry about the peer pressures that lead to destructive behaviors, peer pressure can be equally positive when the peer approval focuses on academic success or encourages participation in plays, sports, clubs, or other activities. Being a member of a social group is, in fact, a vital link in learning successful adult social interactions.

The Role of the Community

In addition to the need for successful peer interaction comes an increased awareness of the broader social world with an accompanying concern for social justice.

The young adolescents' sense of right and wrong is intense. If you want to find a solution to a social problem, give it to a group of middle school students. Their new awareness of the world around them, a need to be involved with their peers, and a mind that is open to all possibilities allow them to seek and act on solutions that are seemingly out of the realm of adult thought. Their new cognitive thinking skills come unimpaired by experiences of failure that often impede adults in devising solutions.

Although parents may be relegated to a lesser role in the influence they hold over their young adolescent children, these same children will listen to and emulate other adults. Whether it be teachers, parents of their friends, or community members, adults have the opportunity to influence and lead the young adolescent in positive directions. Their letter-writing campaigns, canned food drives, volunteering, and political activism provide a wide range of experiences and a sense of empowerment and meaning within the group—all essential elements in young adolescent growth.

The Role of the Media

> The adolescent's world cannot be understood without considering the enormous power of the mass media, especially television, but also movies and popular music. Together with the increasing penetration of cable television, videocassette recorders, and computers in American homes and schools, these electronic conduits for programming and advertising have become strong competitors to the traditional societal institutions in shaping young people's attitudes and values.
>
> CARNEGIE COUNCIL (1996, 41)

The above statement was made a mere four years ago, and as we embrace a new millennium, the Internet, as well, has become a powerful lure for youth. The media in all its forms can have positive or negative effects on the young adolescent. Because they are susceptible to media advertising, young adolescents must become aware of the impact that it has in their lives. Often it is the media that defines for these children whether they are worthy or not—whether they are normal. The media tells them that they are too thin, too fat, too tall, not athletic enough, not hip enough to the latest fashion trends.

The impact of the media cannot and should not be underrated. With access to the World Wide Web increasing, the information flow is unprecedented and endless. Helping young adolescents understand its power as well as its pitfalls, its ability to engage as well as to addict, its wide source of accurate as well as erroneous information, becomes a daunting but vital task for parents and educators.

Despite interest in conforming and belonging to a social group, young adolescents still want individuality. The need for confirmation by a social group is really a need for personal validation.

Emotional Development

The middle school student confronts a diverse number of changes all at one time:

- accepting physical changes
- experiencing new modes of intellectual functioning
- striving for independence from the family
- trying to become a person with a unique identity
- adjusting to a new school setting
- relating to new friends

This period of transition between dependence and independence results in a multitude of needs and a dramatic change in self-concept. The physical changes themselves and the hormones that cause them often trigger emotions that are variable and little understood. Learning to be part of a social group is an important part of the successful transition to independence. More vital, perhaps, are attempts to understand the "self."

When Rob, a fourteen-year-old eighth grader, was asked what the most important thing to learn at school was, he commented, "Not caring what other people think. Most people, if they get made fun of, they'd take it personally. I've learned, and a lot of people make fun of me, that if you don't care, you have a lot more fun because you're not trying to impress people. It's getting your own style." When Rob was asked, however, to comment on the biggest problem facing middle school students, he replied, "Making your presence known." Like other young adolescents, Rob is developing his self-concept and self-esteem. Although we sense that Rob is socially well adjusted, he feels the need to develop a strong sense of identity and begs for personal acceptance as well as the acknowledgment of himself apart from the group—as an individual.

The Search for Identity

> Identity is a patchwork of flesh, feelings and ideas held together by the string of the moment.

RICHARD BORDEAUX (1993)

Erikson's Theories

The search for identity is the defining characteristic of the young adolescent. The first comprehensive look at identity during early adolescence was done by Erik Erikson during the 1950s and 1960s (Erikson 1950, 1968). According to Erikson, during adolescence, individuals struggle to find out who they are and where they are going in life. Young adolescents are just beginning this struggle, trying to integrate their childhood experiences with their developing bodies and biological drives, their new thinking capacities and their ever expanding social roles. This search for identity doesn't begin and end during early adolescence. It involves a slow searching for a lifestyle that is compatible with physical changes, intellectual understandings, and social interactions.

When asked about the greatest problem middle school students experience, Jesse, an eighth grader, responded, "I think it's definitely that people want to fit in—they don't want to stand alone. But I think it's also important to be an individual, too. There are a lot of cliques in middle school. People get into little groups and I think that's bad because you need to stand as an individual."

This search for identity in the young adolescent often revolves around trying out new ideas and behaviors that would have seemed incomprehensible only a year before. It involves looking at situations through different points of view and making decisions about how to act in a given situation in an attempt to develop a public self that is congruent with the inner self and is validated by peers and society. Those decisions, never etched in stone, become the foundation of an identity

29

that is ever changing throughout life. Those not measuring up to cultural and societal expectations may develop negative identities in order to be acknowledged by a peer group and recognized by society.

Identity development poses additional problems for minorities. How does one develop a sense of self within a dominant culture whose values may be contradictory to those of one's personal culture? Not only do minorities and young adolescents of color have to deal with general developmental issues, they must develop an ethnic identity (Gay 1994). Gay indicates, "A clarified ethnic identity is central to the psychosocial well-being and educational success of youth of color" (151). She goes on to say, "If ethnic identity development is understood as part of the natural 'coming of age' process during early adolescence, and if middle level education is to be genuinely client-centered for students of color, then ethnic sensitivity must be incorporated into school policies, programs, and practices" (153).

Teachers must deliberately create learning environments that attend to cultural, ethnic, and racial issues. As we talk about appropriate middle school practices in this book, we will present a framework for curriculum and instruction that responds to these issues.

Marcia's Theory
James Marcia (1980) expanded on Erikson's idea of identity, using the notions of crisis and commitment. *Crisis* is defined as "a period of exploring alternatives" and *commitment* as "making choices." Marcia identifies four resolutions to the search for identity.

1. *Identity diffusion*—no exploration and no commitment. Students neither explore nor choose from the options available to them. They do not question alternatives or act. Someone is making decisions for them. Parents could choose their after-school activities, their friends, and their clothes. This situation is often the case for elementary school children and it is what young adolescents are struggling against.

2. *Identity foreclosure*—commitment without exploration. Here, a choice is made about a lifestyle in the absence of opportunities to explore alternatives. Early maturers who become great

30

athletes in the middle grades may experience identity fore-closure. These students have been defined by their physical precociousness and either have not been given the opportunity to explore other options or have chosen not to.

We should consider that perhaps many of the risk taking and sometimes dangerous behaviors that young adolescents choose to engage in might be the result of their need to explore life and all its options when they feel that their options are being denied. Teachers must be careful about labeling students prematurely; for example as great athletes, musicians, scholars, or leaders, thus denying the opportunity for these students to experience a variety of options for their lives and perhaps denying other students the opportunity to become an athlete, musician, scholar, or leader.

3. *Moratorium*—exploration but no commitment. Students search and explore without making a commitment to a lifestyle. Ideally, middle school students should be at this stage. The existence of options and opportunities allows students to explore areas they might not have considered before. For example, providing musical or athletic opportunities for the late maturer may open a career that expands as maturation unfolds. All students who want to be in plays, sing in the chorus, play in the jazz band, cheer at ball games, or join the science club should be allowed to participate in these activities.

4. *Achievement*—exploration of roles followed by commitment to a specific identity. Identity achievement will not occur during the middle school years. Throughout high school, college, and into early adulthood, opportunities should exist for people to explore options and make decisions and choices about their futures.

For students of color, these stages also become part of the search for an ethnic identity. From little exploration of ethnicity (identity diffusion), to nonexploration in which identity is defined by others (foreclosure), to a time when exploration is embraced (moratorium), to the development of an ethnic identity (achievement), the young adolescent of color must go through a dual process of self-identification and cultural identification (Gay 1994).

Marcia's theory, although not universally accepted, does provide us with a view of how the process of identity development may occur and how we can better help the young adolescent explore the many options the world has to offer. Too often we push students into making choices. We limit opportunities rather than opening them up. We let only the "best" be part of the jazz band or choral group. Only those who demonstrate acting ability can be in the play. When we limit opportunities we pass on the message that a certain student is not capable enough, good enough, strong enough, or smart enough to make a contribution. Our job is to provide opportunities, not deny them. Middle school students should never be told they are inadequate. They just might believe it!

Mood Swings

Eric, a thirteen-year-old seventh grader, was having a particularly rough evening. He had gone to school that morning his typical bouncy self. That evening, he laid around on the couch with his dog at his side, staring into space. Questions by his mom brought monosyllabic responses, "Yes," "No," "Nothing." Pressured by her concern about what was wrong, he finally said to her, thanks to his school's comprehensive health curriculum and class unit on self-esteem, "Don't worry, Mom. I'm an adolescent now. I'm supposed to have mood swings."

Mood swings are a quintessential characteristic of young adolescence. Emotions change rapidly. Students are happy one moment and angry or sad the next; quiet one day and loud and boisterous the next; terrified with respect to one issue and overconfident about another; anxious on Monday and self-assured on Tuesday.

Too often mood swings are blamed on hormones and are discounted as temporary aberrations. Although we can attribute some mood swings to chemical imbalances or rapid fluctuations of hormones, that's only part of it. If we consider the wide social and intellectual changes young adolescents are experiencing, their emotional variability seems understandable.

Behavior Issues

Yes, the search for meaning and identity can be a difficult—even traumatic—experience. Young adolescents face a constant concern about whether they are normal; a dissatisfaction with who they are, how they look, what they believe; a belief that something is wrong with their physical development. It's no wonder that young adolescents exhibit behaviors that seem at times contradictory, bizarre, dangerous, or just plain rude.

Young adolescents can be kind and compassionate and mercilessly cruel. Sensitive to criticism and easily offended, they may become unhappy and take their frustrations out on others: family members, teachers, and especially their classmates. Insults, name calling, and pejorative labeling occur often among students. Celeste, an eighth grader, described one incident between students: "We have some retarded people in this school. A couple of days ago I saw this girl and she was saying, 'Get out of my way you stupid people!' Oh my gosh, that is so mean. I could never say anything like that."

Young adolescents' feelings of inadequacy and attempts to gain control over their constantly changing environments prompt much of their inappropriate behavior. Students find ways of protecting themselves. Lashing out against others is often the chosen path of self-protection. When asked about problems for their age group, Sarah, a seventh grader, reported, "People take it [their frustrations] out on school, their friends, their school life. . . . They make their lives miserable for themselves instead of making them better."

On the other hand, middle schoolers can be intensely loyal to their peers, team, parents, and family. Behavior is also subject to wild fluctuation. One never quite knows what to expect—except for the fact that if we wait a while, it will change.

Self-esteem

Self-esteem often suffers due to the changes young adolescents experience during the middle school years. The self-consciousness that accompanies this stage of growth originates in the young person's perceived loss of control over his or her environment. If students are unable to establish positive feelings about themselves and develop healthy relationships with their peers, young adolescents are likely to feel alienated and may eventually choose to drop out of school (Mills, Dunham, and Alpert 1988). Rob, age fourteen, jokingly tells his friends, teachers, and family, "Seventy percent of middle school kids suffer from low self-esteem and you're contributing to the problem." Rob acknowledges that his statistics may be in error but senses among his peers the need for affirmation and success.

Young adolescence brings with it life's first identity crisis, in which students attempt to project an image consistent with the inner self, which they hope will be accepted by others who make up their world. Young adolescents' concerns are real, their problems are unique to them, and their bravado often masks fear and anxiety. Middle schools must provide opportunities for students to understand the growth they are experiencing and be given chances to exercise their independence in supportive ways. Bessie, a seventh grader, stated the needs of young adolescents quite clearly: "My least favorite thing about school is being told what to do. I think that if you're going to find out what it means to grow up you need to make your own decisions."

Concluding Reflections

This chapter was meant to provide insight into the multitude of changes that young adolescents face throughout their middle school years and the impact of these changes. Keith recalled his middle school experience in a statement he wrote as a college junior. "Overall, as I look back, it [young adolescence] wasn't so bad. Back then, though, I probably would not have agreed with that statement. Every aspect—my friends, family, school, emotional and physical changes—all greatly affected me while I was growing up."

As we work with young adolescents, we must be aware of these changes. It is a time of transition between dependence and independence, a time to explore new alternatives and try out new identities, a time to experiment with new points of view, and a time to learn how to interact with others. Although often seemingly chaotic and confusing, it is their time.

Think about these possibilities:

- What if we truly supported and encouraged young adolescents in their quest to develop a self?
- What if we based schooling on the knowledge of early adolescent development?
- What if we designed a school that acknowledges the physical changes that these students are going through?
- What if we developed a curriculum that responded to their changing intellectual and social worlds?
- What if we provided an environment that supported their need for social interactions and emotional stability?
- What if we listened to what they said?
- What if their questions became our questions?
- What if . . . ?

References

BLACKBURN, JAMES. 1999. Conversation with the authors, West Chester, PA, 12 March.

BORDEAUX, R. 1993–1994. Unpublished poetry for class project. Sinte Gleska University, Mission, SD.

CAINE, R. N., AND G. CAINE. 1994. *Making Connections: Teaching and the Human Brain.* Menlo Park, CA: Addison Wesley.

CARNEGIE COUNCIL ON ADOLESCENT DEVELOPMENT. 1996. *Great Transitions: Preparing Adolescents for a New Century.* Abridged version. New York: Carnegie Corporation of New York.

ERIKSON, E. H. 1950. *Childhood and Society.* New York: W. W. Norton.

———. 1968. *Identity: Youth and Crisis.* New York: W. W. Norton.

GAY, G. 1994. "Coming of Age Ethnically: Teaching Young Adolescents of Color." *Theory Into Practice* 33 (3): 149–155.

LOUNSBURY, J., AND D. CLARK. 1990. *Inside Grade Eight: From Apathy to Excitement.* Reston, VA: National Association of Secondary School Principals.

MARCIA, J. 1980. "Ego Identity Development." In *The Handbook of Adolescent Psychology*, ed. J. Adelson. New York: Wiley, 159–187.

MILGRAM, J. 1992. "A Portrait of Diversity: The Middle Level Student." In *Transforming Middle Level Education: Perspectives and Possibilities*, ed. J. L. Irvin. Needham Heights, MA: Allyn and Bacon, 16–27.

MILLS, R. C., R. G. DUNHAM, AND G. P. ALPERT. 1988. "Working with High-Risk Young in Prevention and Early Intervention Programs: Toward a Comprehensive Wellness Model." *Adolescence* 23: 643–660.

NOTTELMANN, E. D., E. J. SUSMAN, J. H. BLUE, G. INOFF-GERMAIN, L. D. DORN, D. L. LORIAUX, G. B. CUTLER, AND G. P. CHROUSOS. 1987. "Gonadal and Adrenal Hormone Correlates of Adjustment in Early Adolescence." In *Biological-Psychological Interacts in Early Adolescence*, eds. R. M. Lerner and T. T. Foch. Hillsdale, NJ: Erlbaum.

PETERSEN, A. C. 1987. "Those Gangly Years." *Psychology Today*, September, 28–34.

PIAGET, J. 1977a. *The Development of Thought: Elaboration of Cognitive Structures*. New York: Viking.

———. 1977b. *The Essential Piaget*. New York: Basic Books.

RICE, R. P. 1999. *The Adolescent: Development, Relationships, and Culture*. Needham Heights, MA: Allyn and Bacon.

SANTROCK, J. W. AND S. R. YUSSEN. 1992. *Child Development: An Introduction*. Dubuque, IA: William C. Brown Publishers.

SIMMONS, R. G., AND D. A. BLYTH. 1987. *Moving into Adolescence*. New York: Aldine de Gruyter.

TANNER, J. M. 1972. "Sequence, Tempo and Individual Variation in Growth and Development of Boys and Girls Aged Twelve to Sixteen." In *Twelve to Sixteen*, eds. J. Kagan and R. Coles. New York: W. W. Norton, 1–23.

VAN HOOSE, J., AND D. STRAHAN. 1988. *Young Adolescent Development and School Practices: Promoting Harmony*. Columbus, OH: National Middle School Association.

WRIGHT, M. R. 1989. "Body Image Satisfaction in Adolescent Girls and Boys." *Journal of Youth and Adolescence* 18: 71–84.

THREE

Influences from the Past and the Present

Middle school is like a prison.

RYAN, SIXTH GRADER

You wake up early, you work all day at school, and then, they expect you to do homework.

ELIZABETH, SEVENTH GRADER

The above statements reveal what many young adolescents think of their middle schools. Students are often given numerous and lengthy homework assignments that they may not be able to comprehend. They are expected to take notes during a lecture that has no meaning for them. In some schools, students have few if any opportunities for social interaction during the school day. Recess typically has been eliminated from the middle school day despite the overwhelming need  for physical activity among young adolescents. Student involvement in curricular or instructional decisions seldom exists despite young adolescents' hypersensitivity to life's global issues and an understanding of their own learning characteristics and needs. Maybe school *is* like a prison! As some middle school educators begin to change school structures to meet the needs of their students, other teachers and principals persist in maintaining traditional structures that are inappropriate for young adolescents.

Time for Reflection

- As you reflect on the developmental characteristics of young adolescents discussed in Chapter 2, brainstorm with your classmates how a middle school could respond to the developmental needs of young adolescents.
- Work collaboratively with others in this class to write a description of what an ideal middle school would be like based on your understanding of young adolescent development learning characteristics and needs.

A Typical Day

> I feel like a cow. They herd us in the building in the morning trying to fit a thousand kids in two doors. Then they make us get into our stalls. Then they make us get into line and serve us all the same food. Then they give us fifteen minutes of pasture time after lunch; then herd us back into the classroom.
>
> ROB, EIGHTH GRADER

The school bus arrives at the street corner at 7:25 A.M. Students arrive at school at 8:10 following a forty-five minute bus ride. Upon entering the school, they are ushered into the gymnasium to sit quietly for ten minutes until the homeroom bell rings, allowing them to go into the hallway to their lockers.

Students enter a long hallway filled with lockers that stand inches apart from one another. Three hundred students share the hallway at the same time attempting to get into their lockers and avoid bumping into one another. Students with adjacent lockers are not able to get to them at the same time because of the close proximity. Lockers are only twenty centimeters wide, thus slowing the process of attempting to cram into them coats, band instruments, and all those books and note-books required by each teacher. Added to this confusion is the fact that students are allowed only three, maybe four, minutes to open their lock-ers and take out the appropriate materials for their first few classes.

Classes begin and students sit passively for forty-two minutes as they listen to a lecture, complete worksheets, answer questions in the back of the textbook chapter, or take written tests. As the bell rings at the end of each period, students file into the crowded hallway and play the locker game again, jostling for position to assure arrival at their next class on time. Finally, after three hours of classes, they have a lunch period.

The lunch line is long because everyone realizes that it's not cool to bring your lunch anymore. Lunch periods are a short twenty to twenty-five minutes (a time frame that prevents students from becom-ing too loud). If students are in the back of the line, by the time they sit down they will have about seven minutes to eat. The lunch menu is determined by administrators and does not allow for student choice. Lunchtime presents the only opportunity for socializing that students will have until after school on the bus ride home. Those students who don't have enough time to eat their whole lunch won't get a chance to eat again until after school.

Students head back to class after lunch without any opportunity for physical exercise except an occasional run down the long hallway before teachers arrive at their posts. Some students feel exhausted after eating lunch, as they return to the classrooms for three more forty-two minute-classes.

Each of the five teachers the students see assigns evening home-work. Students need thirty minutes to an hour or more to complete the homework for each class. They are afforded few opportunities for so-cializing, physical exercise, or discussing their concerns and interests each day. Finally, students board the bus for a forty-five-minute trip home. If they begin their homework soon after they arrive home, they may complete it by 10:00 P.M., provided they don't spend any time talking to friends, exercising, or just hanging out for an hour or so.

Does the description conjure up fond memories of your own past experiences? Is this an appropriate way to educate young adolescents? What events caused the design of such a stifling environment for students? Throughout the past hundred years, several factors have influenced the design of the public school day, but perhaps the most severe influence has been the attempt by educators to emulate the factory model of private industry.

Emulating the Factory

Several societal forces have affected teachers' perceptions of their roles and have been instrumental in the way teachers provide instruction and make curricular decisions. The development of the assembly line in factories in the early 1900s had an enormous impact on the structure of education. Factories were designed so that each person had a specific job to do and performed the same task all day long. Work started and ended with the blast of a horn or a bell. Breaks were granted to workers on a set timetable. Work was evaluated by the amount of time on task and the number of items produced each day. The boss's job was to keep the employees on task. Reflective thinking among the workers on the assembly line was not necessarily required and certainly not valued. Bosses wanted compliant employees who were highly productive during long hours on the job. They did not expect employees to question the work they were responsible for completing or how it was done.

During the early 1900s, schools were "concerned with producing a work force to staff and operate the factories" (Caine and Caine 1994, 13). Hence, schools used the factory model to design their structure. Schools contrived a seven- or eight-period day, with classes lasting approximately forty to forty-five minutes, ending with a bell as students filed out of their classes, into the halls for four minutes, and then into another classroom. Subjects were taught separately, and all of the outcomes for learning were predetermined by textbook design or pre-structured curriculum chosen by central office administrators. Every student was expected to learn the same curriculum, at the same pace, and all students were taught in the same way. Compliant behavior was rewarded; creative and critical thinking were discouraged.

Influence on Teaching Beliefs

When education is designed according to the factory model, students are treated as raw materials whose entrance through the "factory door" leads to attempts to mold and polish them into something new without regard to the needs or variations of the original material. Several assumptions are implicit in this design:

1. All students have similar learning characteristics.
2. Teaching is a simple process whereby one style fits the needs of all students.
3. The amount of information students need to learn has an established limit.
4. The information that students are expected to know is unilaterally predetermined and involves a fixed set of concepts and principles.
5. All students are expected to perform similar responsibilities once they graduate.
6. Learning means memorization of facts.
7. Creative and critical thinking are not valued.
8. Connections do not exist between subjects.
9. Teachers are the unilateral decision makers with respect to events that occur in the classroom.

These assumptions ignore what researchers are discovering about cognition and the learning process, and they ignore what is known about young adolescent development.

So what is it about the factory model that influenced middle schools? You may be saying, "That was then. Look at us now." Look around you! Do schools continue to deliver information in forty-two-minute segments? Is the school day divided into seven or eight periods? Are subjects taught separately? If so, you are experiencing the factory model of schooling.

Teachers may have a difficult time envisioning a schooling structure that looks different from the factory model. They often hold tightly to traditional views of learning because for many it's all they've ever experienced. Many parents expect schools to continue using the same teaching and learning processes for their children that they experienced (Brown and Rose 1995). These predominant belief systems create a challenging barrier for those administrators, teachers, and university professors who are interested in implementing needed change.

Influence on Teacher Behaviors

The factory model approach not only affects educators' choice of instructional strategies but also student socialization, student/teacher relationships, and the general quality of schooling for many at-risk students. The factory model prevents teachers from developing the kind of caring relationships with students that are required as a basis for learning. Researchers (Caine and Caine 1994) who understand the relationship between emotion and cognitive processing have warned us of the negative effects of a sterile learning environment. Positive feelings associated with learning experiences foster meaningful learning. Forty-two minutes is not sufficient for enabling teachers to develop the kind of healthy, caring relationships with students that are necessary to promote meaningful learning. Adam, an eighth grader, describes one aspect of his "perfect" middle school: "Teachers would be friendly with the kids. Some are okay, but the teachers aren't close enough to kids." When students and teachers have opportunities and time to communicate with one other, they begin to care about each other in ways that make meaningful learning possible. Edith, a sixth-grade teacher, explained, "I definitely think the middle school should be more nurturing. I find my role as a teacher is just one part of it. I feel like I am a counselor, a grandmother; it's much more than just teaching."

Similarly, forty-two-minute periods prevent teachers from identifying the cognitive needs of all of their students, thus denying educators an opportunity to design curricula and instructional strategies in a way that ensures optimal learning. Forty-two-minute periods limit opportunities to complete curricula in a meaningful manner; instead, teachers are encouraged to briefly cover topics in an attempt to move to another topic each day and therefore complete the book. Sheila, a seventh grader, had this to say about the traditional lecture-style classroom: "Civics is so boring. We read our book and we do these answer-and-question pages. We never do anything as a whole class—we just read and take notes the whole time."

Students need longer blocks of time for meaningful learning to occur. They need opportunities to construct their own knowledge through discovery, to formulate and ask questions, to engage in in-depth problem solving, and to use critical and creative thinking processes. When these actions occur, students are involved in active learning experiences. An eighth grader, Meg, put it this way: "We need fun ways to learn and more challenges. We need to expand our minds."

The factory model of schooling limits quality socialization among students. Short periods, four minutes between classes, large numbers of students in each class, predetermined curricular guidelines—these are but a few of the structures that discourage teachers from using collaborative learning experiences in their lesson design. In recognizing the social needs of young adolescents, teachers should design opportunities for students to learn collaboratively. Cooperative learning strategies take more time to initially implement, and short class periods may discourage teachers from using them. Edith, a sixth grade teacher, was in a middle school that moved to longer blocks of time for each period. She commented, "This year I started a double whole language period and then a math—it was fabulous. From 8:15 until 9:45 I have the same children. This is really advantageous to the students."

When students are forced to learn as much material as is expected in a seven-period school day, it is unlikely that teachers will provide time for young adolescents' much needed physical activities. Teachers who work in schools that follow the factory model design lessons filled with content material that make the best use of forty-two minutes. Although many administrators and parents may applaud this type of time-on-task rigor that characterized education in the 1980s, young adolescents are unlikely to be paying attention to the lessons anyway because of their pent-up energy and physical discomfort.

The negative effects of schools that emulated the factory were noted by students interviewed by Lounsbury and Johnston (1988).

These researchers asked sixth grade students what they would change about their middle school if they could. Their responses included the following:

- more time at lunch
- later starting times for school
- less homework
- opportunities to eat in class
- bigger lockers

Based on what is now known about how learning occurs and the developmental abilities and needs of young adolescents, middle schools must abandon the factory model approach to schooling and evolve into more effective centers of learning. A few schools have recognized the needs of young adolescents and replaced the factory model with more developmentally appropriate structures. These structural and philosophical changes began to be incorporated in middle level schools thirty years ago.

The First Junior High Schools

The first junior high schools were not necessarily designed to account for the needs of their students. The most common organizational pattern of education in the late 1800s was eight years at an elementary school and, if students were continuing their education past that—few were—high school. In 1893 concern about the inconsistencies in college preparation resulted in the formation of an organization of educators known as The Committee of Ten on Secondary School Studies (Gruhn and Douglass 1971). This committee recommended that secondary school begin in the seventh grade. The division into six years of elementary school and six years of high school lasted until 1909, when concern about the immaturity of sixth grade students and overcrowding of high schools led to the development of the first seventh-through-ninth-grade school in Columbus, Ohio. This school was recognized as the junior high school. In 1919 the North Central Association of Colleges and Secondary Schools provided a definition of the junior high: "A junior high school is a school in which the seventh, eighth, and ninth grades are segregated in a building (or portion of a building) by themselves; possess an organization and administration of their own that is distinct from the grades above and below, and are taught by a separate corps of teachers" (North Central Association 4).

The junior high was originally designed to provide a program that would respond to the uniqueness of this developmental stage and offer a practical and active curriculum that would engage the young adolescent mind (Tye 1985). The junior high school curricula, however, were heavily influenced by the development and use of Carnegie Units in high schools around 1910 (Toepfer 1992). Carnegie units are credits awarded for completing high school courses and were developed as a means of measuring the number of courses that students would be required to complete in high school in order to graduate. Junior high school faculty were concerned that students needed to be prepared for ninth grade. Therefore, they chose the Carnegie Unit structure in an effort to bolster junior high school students' academic preparedness for high school.

False Hope

Approximately 6,500 junior high schools existed across the country by the 1950s. Despite its popularity and the rhetoric of developmental appropriateness that accompanied its initiation, the junior high school never quite lived up to its promise of providing a distinct experience for young adolescents. Many junior highs were and currently are staffed by teachers with little or no knowledge of young adolescent development who lack the strategies needed for meeting students' cognitive, social, and emotional needs (McEwin, Dickinson, and Jenkins 1996). Instead of developing practical and active curricula, junior high schools maintained traditional content-specific curricula and a factory model design of six forty-two-minute periods throughout the day.

Throughout the 1940s and 1950s the need for a distinct educational experience for young adolescents remained in the forefront of the minds of many educators and developmentalists. These educators suggested

that junior high schools provide curricula designed for student exploration and integration of knowledge and that the schools at this level
provide many opportunities for socialization. It was the Association for
Supervision and Curriculum Development (ASCD) that responded to
these calls for change in 1961 with the publication of *The Junior High
School We Need* (Grantes, Noyce, Patterson, and Robertson 1961).
The authors envisioned a school in which educators were specifically
trained to use appropriate instructional strategies to teach young adolescents. They recommended smaller schools with flexible scheduling
formats rather than the traditional forty-two-minute, six-period day.
The authors' suggestions, unfortunately, were not implemented widely
until the 1990s.

The Promise of a New Design

"What if?" some educators were asking. "What if we actually attempted
to respond to the needs of young adolescents? What if we developed a
school with the characteristics proposed by the Association for Supervision and Curriculum Development?" Fueled by powerful convic-
tions, in the mid-1960s the middle school concept began to develop in
some communities: Upper St. Clair, Pennsylvania; Centerville, Ohio;
and Barrington, Illinois (George, Stevenson, Thomason, and Beane
1992). In Upper St. Clair, one of the school districts where the name
"junior high" was changed to "middle school," assistant superintendent
Donald Eichhorn not only talked about the need for restructuring, he
was instrumental in creating a new middle school structure. As such,
"He shook not only Upper St. Clair; he shook the nations' middle
level schools and put into motion a process in Pennsylvania which led
to the recognition of the middle grades as a distinctive level in K–12
education" (Brough 1994, 19). Eichhorn redefined instructional practice, established advisory programs to meet students' emotional needs,
and developed multiage grouping for students. Perhaps his greatest ac-
complishment was his courageous willingness to question the validity
of the existing traditional curricular structure. Although more middle
schools were created throughout the United States shortly after the

Upper St. Clair innovation, most of these were middle schools in name only.

Demographic Influences on Middle School Development

Many junior highs that changed their names to "middle school" did so because of demographic factors that occurred when baby boomers completed high school and a small "baby boomlet" flooded the elementary grades with overwhelming numbers of new students (George et al. 1992). Suddenly classrooms were available in high school buildings and a shortage of classrooms existed in kindergarten-through-sixth-grade buildings. The school board's solution was to move the ninth graders into the high school, move the sixth and sometimes fifth graders into the junior high, and rename the junior high the "middle school." Schools in other areas of the United States also began moving to the middle school design due to the mandate to desegregate schools (George, et al.).

Unfortunately, the unrealistic academic expectations required of these new students—specifically sixth graders—was as intense as that previously expected of seventh and eighth graders. Again, these were middle schools in name only—not in their design or in the ways in which students' developmental needs were addressed. Middle schools of the 1960s and 1970s utilized features common to high schools, such as departmentalized instruction, forty-two-minute periods, and tracking of students according to ability—in essence, the factory model approach to educating students.

Support for Genuine Middle Schools

The National Middle School Association (NMSA), founded in 1973, began to advocate for the needs of middle school students on a national level. NMSA published a position paper entitled *This We Believe* in 1982 to publicize the importance of recognizing the unique developmental needs of young adolescents. The authors of this report asserted that simply designating an institution a "middle school" was not enough to meet the needs of young adolescents; schools must also be responsive to developmental issues.

The Carnegie Corporation of New York established the Carnegie Council on Adolescent Development in 1986 out of concern for the high risks for drug and alcohol abuse, early pregnancy, school failure, and violence that adolescents faced. This group's task was to develop strategies to meet the needs of adolescents in a rapidly changing environment. Although many middle level educators continued to develop appropriate programs for their students, on a national level the education reform movement of the 1980s failed to provide specific suggestions for improving schools for young adolescents. Education became a central focus of the Carnegie Council: it established the Task Force on the Education of Young Adolescents. One role of the task force members was to determine why middle schools and junior high schools were not meeting the needs of young adolescents. The group reported the following:

- Middle and junior high schools contained large enrollments.
- The students had developed few meaningful relationships with the adults in the schools (teachers, administrators, counselors); that is, the adults did not become well acquainted with the students.
- The chosen curricula were irrelevant to students.
- The majority of instructional strategies used were better suited for specialized classes of the high school or college.

The task force developed a proposal for educators and parents to suggest the design of a school that would better meet middle school students' needs. The group's report, published in 1989, was titled *Turning Points: Preparing Youth for the 21st Century* (Carnegie Council on Adolescent Development 1989). Hamburg, chair of the council, provided this descriptive comment about young adolescents and the responsibility that schools had to these students:

The emerging adolescent is caught in turbulence, a fascinated but perplexed observer of the biological, psychological, and social changes swirling all around. In groping for a solid path toward a worthwhile adult life, adolescents can grasp the middle grade school as the crucial and reliable handle. Now, the middle grade school must change, and change substantially, to cope with the requirements of a new era—to give students a decent chance in life and to help them fulfill their youthful promise. (14)

Task force members identified the kind of person they wanted middle schools to turn out. This would be

- an intellectually reflective person
- a person enroute to a lifetime of meaningful work
- a good citizen
- a caring and ethical individual
- a healthy person. (*Turning Points* 1989, 15)

The Carnegie task force members provided eight recommendations that have become basic guidelines for developing an appropriate educational setting for young adolescents. These recommendations form the core of what is known as the "middle school concept."

A seven-year longitudinal study of middle schools implementing these recommendations indicates significant academic and social growth, with students scoring higher than state norms on mathematics, language arts, and reading assessments. Improvements were also found in student behavior (Felner et al. 1997). This study is discussed at length in Chapter 9. Following is the executive summary of the task force's recommendations (1989):

1. *Create small communities for learning* where stable, close, mutually respectful relationships with adults and peers are considered fundamental for intellectual development and personal growth. The key elements of these communities are schools-within-schools or houses, students and teachers grouped together as teams, and small group advisories that ensure that every student is well known by at least one adult.

2. *Teach a core academic program* that results in students who are literate, including in the sciences, and who know how to think

critically, lead a healthy life, behave ethically, and assume the responsibilities of citizenship in a pluralistic society. Youth service to promote values for citizenship is an essential part of the core academic program.

3. *Ensure success for all students* through the elimination of tracking by achievement level and promotion of cooperative learning, flexibility in arranging instructional time, and adequate resources (time, space, equipment, and materials) for teachers.

4. *Empower teachers and administrators to make decisions about the experiences of middle grade students* through creative control by teachers over the instructional program linked to greater responsibilities for students' performance, governance committees that assist the principal in designing and coordinating school-wide programs, and autonomy and leadership within subschools or houses to create environments tailored to enhance the intellectual and emotional development of all youth.

5. *Staff middle grade schools with teachers who are expert at teaching young adolescents* and who have been specifically prepared for assignment to the middle grades.

6. *Improve academic performance through fostering the health and fitness* of young adolescents, by providing a health coordinator in every middle grade school, access to health care and counseling services, and a health-promoting school environment.

7. *Reengage families in the education of young adolescents* by giving families meaningful roles in school governance, communicating with families about the school program and students' progress, and offering families opportunities to support the learning process at home and at the school.

8. *Connect schools with communities*, which together share responsibilities for each middle grade students' success, through identifying service opportunities in the community, establishing partnerships and collaborations to ensure students' access to health and social services, and using community resources to enrich the instructional program and opportunities for constructive after-school activities. (9–10)

Researchers from NMSA followed shortly after with a revised edition of *This We Believe* (1992). This report described the characteristics of developmentally responsive middle schools.

The National Middle School Association believes: Developmentally responsive middle level schools are characterized by:

- educators committed to young adolescents
- a shared vision
- high expectations for all
- an adult advocate for every student
- family and community partnerships
- a positive school climate

Therefore, developmentally responsive middle level schools provide:

- curriculum that is challenging, integrative, and exploratory
- varied teaching and learning approaches
- assessment and evaluation that promote learning
- flexible organizational structures
- programs and policies that foster health, wellness, and safety
- comprehensive guidance and support services

(NMSA 11)

Throughout this book we will describe many of the Carnegie Council and NMSA ideas in detail. Increasingly, their recommendations for appropriate practices are being implemented by middle schools across the nation. One of our purposes in writing this book is to explain the reason for and significance of designing middle schools sensitive to the developmental stages and needs of young adolescents. We sincerely hope that preservice and inservice teachers will initiate the development of more effective middle schools once they understand the significance of these suggested changes. The courage and actions of teachers change schooling more than the efforts of administrators or professors who write books! It is imperative that teachers comprehend their role and assume responsibility for improving middle level education. We hope this book will enable you to become an agent of change at your middle school.

> **Time for Reflection**
> - Return to the middle school design you devised at the start of this chapter. Compare your group's design with the thoughts put forth by NMSA and the Carnegie Report.
> - Decide as a group how you would alter your design or change the design suggested by the NMSA and the Carnegie Report.

References

BROUGH, J. A. 1994. "Donald H. Eichhorn: Pioneer in Inventing Schools for Transescents." *Middle School Journal* 25, no. 4: 19–22.

BROWN, D. F., AND T. D. ROSE. 1995. "Self-reported Classroom Impact of Teachers' Theories About Learning and Obstacles to Implementation." *Action in Teacher Education* 27, no. 1: 20–29.

CARNEGIE COUNCIL ON ADOLESCENT DEVELOPMENT. 1989. *Turning Points: Preparing American Youth for the 21st Century*. New York: Carnegie Corporation.

CAINE, R. N., AND G. CAINE. 1994. *Making Connections: Teaching and the Human Brain*. Menlo Park, CA: Addison Wesley.

FELNER, R. D., L. D. JACKSON, D. KASAK, P. MULHALL, S. BRAND, AND N. FLOWERS. 1997. "The Impact of School Reform for the Middle Years: Longitudinal Study of a Network Engaged in *Turning Points*–Based Comprehensive School Transformation." *Phi Delta Kappan* 78, no. 7: 528–532, 541–550.

GEORGE, P. S., C. STEVENSON, J. THOMASON, AND J. BEANE. 1992. *The Middle School—and Beyond*. Alexandria, VA: Association for Supervision and Curriculum Development.

GRANTES, J. C. NOYCE, F. PATTERSON, AND J. ROBERTSON. 1961. *The Junior High We Need*. Washington, DC: Association for Supervision and Curriculum Development.

GRUHN, W., AND H. DOUGLASS. 1971. *The Modern Junior High School.* 3rd ed. New York: Ronald Press.

LOUNSBURY, J., AND H. JOHNSTON. 1988. *Life in the Three Sixth Grades.* Reston, VA: National Association of Secondary School Principals.

McEWIN, C. K., T. S. DICKINSON, AND D. M. JENKINS. 1996. *America's Middle Schools: Practices and Progress: A 25 Year Perspective.* Columbus, OH: National Middle School Association.

NATIONAL MIDDLE SCHOOL ASSOCIATION. 1992. *This We Believe: Developmentally Responsive Middle Level Schools.* 2d ed. Columbus, OH: National Middle School Association.

NORTH CENTRAL ASSOCIATION. 1919. *Bulletin.* North Central Association of Colleges and Secondary Schools.

TOEPFER, C., Jr. 1992. "Middle Level School Curriculum: Defining the Elusive." In *Transforming Middle Level Education: Perspectives and Possibilities,* ed. J. L. Irvin. Needham Heights, MA: Allyn and Bacon, 205–243.

TYE, K. 1985. *The Junior High: School in Search of a Mission.* New York: University Press of America.

FOUR

Creating a Safe Haven for Learning

Teachers wear a lot of different hats: teacher, doctor, social worker. With middle school age [students], you're wearing all of the hats— almost equally. I find myself playing an advising role all day long.

RODNEY, EIGHTH-GRADE TEACHER

Any student will tell you that teachers cannot feign caring and believing in students. Your students know what you feel about them. A student from an urban middle school reveals this awareness: "Some teachers don't have respect for us. They only come here to get paid. If they don't want to teach they shouldn't be here" (Naima, seventh grader). Every student you teach will realize your commitment to teaching and be aware of the extent of your interest. Students have an entire class period to "size up" teachers to decide whether they should cooperate with them or engage in learning with them.

You may be saying at this point, "I don't need to read this chapter. Of course I care about students, or I wouldn't consider being a professional educator!" You might be surprised by the kind of teacher behaviors and school policies that deflate students' attitudes and confidence. Middle level classrooms aren't always the caring learning havens that you would expect.

Time for Reflection
- Develop a list of characteristics that describe the best teachers you have known.
- Compare your list with others.
- Write a description of the classroom where you learned the most as a student. Consider how students treated each other, how the teacher treated students, and what a typical day was like in that classroom.

Middle Schools and Student Stress

Many situations initiated by teachers can cause fear and stress in young adolescents:

1. frequently yelling at one student or an entire class
2. applying punishment inappropriately
3. threatening students
4. making fun of students
5. establishing unrealistic academic demands or expectations
6. requiring students to open their lockers, get the appropriate books and notebooks, and get to their next class on time—all in less than four minutes
7. pushing students to learn abstract principles that are beyond their cognitive capabilities
8. assigning extensive homework that requires at least an hour or more of work each evening for each subject
9. embarrassing students in front of their most significant audience—their peers.

We've named only a few of the potentially threatening situations that teachers instigate every day for many middle schoolers. We know you're thinking, "I'd never do any of these things." Additionally, through subtle actions, teachers may unwittingly disrupt the emotional stability students require in order for learning to occur:

1. refusing to lend a pencil, protractor, or paper to students
2. caring more about completing the textbook than meeting each student's needs
3. treating each student the same regardless of differences in learning abilities or learning styles
4. preventing students from interacting socially during class time
5. assessing student learning in only one way
6. designing lessons that are primarily teacher-directed without hands-on opportunities for student learning
7. refusing to be flexible in curriculum design, instructional processes, or scheduling
8. using quizzes to "catch" students who may not understand material
9. ignoring young adolescents' stages of cognitive, social, and emotional growth.

Understand that these negative actions affect more than students' self-esteem.

How Stress Affects Student Learning

Anxiety and stress affect the quality of students' cognitive processing, disrupting their ability to process information efficiently. Caine and Caine (1994) describe what many students experience in classrooms perceived as threatening as a "narrowing of the perceptual field" (69). Students are likely to feel a sense of helplessness whenever a situation becomes threatening. Helplessness is followed by a loss of effective cognitive processing, described as "downshifting" (69). When stress associated with fear creates anxiety, people drift into a downshifted state resulting in an inability to use higher-order cognitive abilities efficiently and the inability "to see the interconnectedness . . . among topics" (70). Caine and Caine add that stress-related issues prevent our brains from forming permanent new memories. A number of studies have identified the relationship between socioemotional states of mind and cognition (Elias et al. 1997; Perry 1996; Brendtro, Brokenleg, and Van Bockern 1990). These studies indicate that "under conditions of real or imagined threat or anxiety, there is a loss of focus on the learning process and a reduction in task focus and flexible problem solving" (Elias et al., 3).

Many students consider schools to be the central, if not the only, place where a safe and trusting environment exists. One student from an urban middle school commented: "Students in our school have pressure in the homes and stuff. They can't concentrate in school because at home they've got to be the adult. When they come here [to school], they've got to be the child" (Karen, eighth grader). Even in high socioeconomic communities, schools can be a safe haven for students who are not getting sufficient emotional support at home. A sixth grade teacher, Edith, who teaches in a wealthy neighborhood, spoke of the "emotional needs" of her students despite their high socioeconomic standing: "Because parents are so busy with their jobs, the children are neglected. Someone's not there to listen to them. There's an emotional component within these children that we have to be aware of."

Establishing a Caring Environment

Young adolescents, in moving away from the need for parental approval, need to know that someone other than their peers will provide a support system for them. This comment from an eighth grade male student at an urban school emphasizes the importance of the teacher/student relationship:

> It's not supposed to just be, 'I'm your teacher; I see you in school and that's all.' It should be like a friend bond also; so you can talk to that teacher—be open to her. That way, they get to know more about you.
>
> JOHN, EIGHTH GRADER

According to Elias et al. (1997), "Caring happens when children sense that the adults in their lives think they are important and when they understand that they will be accepted and respected, regardless of any particular talents they have" (6).

Researchers in one study discovered that showing care and respect for students "promoted learning and overpowered the comparative effects of instructional methodologies" (Goodman, Sutton, and Harkevy 1995, 696). Lipsitz (1995) adds: "caring did not substitute for learning; caring established an effective culture for learning" (666). When caring attitudes are demonstrated by teachers, "trust is established and caring interpersonal relationships are built in classrooms" (Chaskin and Mendley Rauner 1995, 673). Creating a caring environment should be a primary initiative for all teachers.

In an interview study with young adolescents, Bosworth (1995) asked students to describe caring teachers. Students reported that caring teachers:

- walk[ed] around the room talking to everybody to see how they were doing [and] to answer questions
- help[ed] students with school work
- noticed and inquired about changes in behavior
- recognized different learning styles and speeds
- sought to know students as unique human beings
- showed respect for students through actions such as "talking in a quiet voice or talking to you in private or alone"
- [did] a good job of explaining the content area, making sure that all students understand
- encourage[d] students to improve. (691–692)

This sounds like a great deal of work to accomplish on a daily basis—and it is. Behind all of these suggestions, however, is probably one of the primary reasons we become teachers: because we really care about students—especially young adolescents!

When teachers show their acceptance of students, and students begin to see and understand that teachers care, school can be mutually satisfying to both students and teachers. You can show students you care by demonstrating several other behaviors:

- sharing your life experiences with students and conveying your excitement for learning
- modeling one-on-one active listening
- helping students develop personal academic and social out-comes
- participating in daily activities such as lunch, recess, and after-school intramurals
- taking the time to discover what is important to your students outside of school—hobbies, interests, family stories, pets
- attending your students' musical, athletic, and theatrical per-formances.

Naturally, you'll think of many other actions once you get to know your students. Some teachers make it a point to spend the first and last few minutes of each class session just talking to students about their personal lives.

Genuinely Knowing Students

Barth (1991) proclaimed, "What needs to be improved about schools is their culture, the quality of interpersonal relationships, and the nature and quality of learning experiences" (45). Teachers are responsible for creating the kinds of interpersonal relationships with students that can improve the quality of learning.

You can test your personal knowledge of your students after the first month of the school year by writing down their names, then listing observations about each of them. Once a personal link with each student is established, you will notice that students begin to focus more effectively on academic issues and learn in more meaningful ways.

Remember that a caring relationship begins with the development of trust and mutual respect between students and teachers. Your job is to create that trust and to maintain a level of respect for each student throughout the year. Respect for students is demonstrated through your modeling of politeness, courtesy, and honesty. Respect is shared between students and teachers when teachers make it a point to recognize students for their efforts and talents—and not merely their academic abilities.

It is imperative to understand that teachers and students *together* have the responsibility for assuring that a classroom is a place in which all students have an opportunity to learn. In developing this collaborative environment, teachers must invite student cooperation. A more traditional view of a teacher's role is as one who controls students' behaviors. Teachers do not control students! Students merely choose to cooperate with us. We suggest that you develop the kind of meaningful connection with each student that encourages students to want to cooperate with you and others. The beauty of establishing a mutually respectful classroom is that it enables students and teachers to reach a common outcome—a comfortable and meaningful learning community.

Developing a respectful community in a school and classroom also includes establishing ground rules for how students treat each other. Most middle school teachers realize, if you don't recall from your own middle school years, that students can be unkind to one another. Teachers have a responsibility to assist students in the challenges they face in responding to daily social pressures.

Encouraging Positive Student Relationships

Young adolescents must don a strong suit of armor when they interact with peers. You can probably recall your own middle school days and the way you were treated by classmates who were your friends one day and your enemies the next. Middle school's social battlefields may best be described as a place of survival of the fittest, and many students don't have the strong social strategies they need to defend themselves. Adults who don't regularly see young adolescents together may not understand the many ways that middle school students can hurt each other through their words and actions. Every middle school teacher has seen the havoc that young adolescents can create socially and emotionally for other students. Although many teachers may believe that it is not in their domain to settle student-to-student conflicts, wise educators take a more proactive role in ensuring that middle level students are polite to one another. Teachers, at least within their classrooms, have a responsibility to provide a safe and secure environment for social interaction among students.

For most students, middle school presents an entirely new social setting in which they see few of their elementary school friends. Young adolescents who enter middle school as fifth or sixth graders usually begin to establish relationships with many new students from varying demographic backgrounds. Creating safe havens for learning begins with designing classroom activities at the beginning of the year that allow students to interact with one another for the purpose of feeling comfortable together. Until students begin to share aspects of their lives with others, they will not experience the sense of trust needed to cooperate with one another or with the teacher.

Safe and secure classrooms are social environments in which teachers provide opportunities for students to become acquainted with one another and with you as the teacher. Teachers should begin the school year with activities that encourage student-to-student interaction, such as

- inviting students to share their life histories
- having students meet in pairs to write newspaper reports describing one of their classmates to the rest of the class
- creating cooperative base groups in each class, in which four students work together and accept responsibility for one another's understanding of material and completion of assignments
- pairing students for safe travel between classes
- helping students learn and practice conflict resolution strategies.

Many books are available that provide teachers with ideas for student team-building activities. Kagan's (1994) book on cooperative learning presents numerous valuable strategies for teachers.

Another primary responsibility for teachers is establishing and enforcing appropriate behavioral expectations. Middle level teachers can frequently be involved in preventing students from embarrassing each other or inflicting emotional pain. Teachers and students together can develop a set of appropriate social expectations in each classroom and enforce those expectations when violations occur. Taking responsibility for enforcement assures that your classroom can be a place of mutual respect and a safe haven for learning. Charney (1991) values the actions of teachers in creating a community classroom environment because of her belief that "part of our mission is to create communities with fewer nightmares, where self-control and care for others minimizes the possibilities of violence" (17). A peaceful classroom environment is a place where students care about and support each other through their daily interactions.

Encouraging Risk Taking

You are responsible as an educator for at least attempting to ensure the success of all of your students—to encourage the development of higher levels of motivation and commitment toward their own growth. A part of this challenge is to invite the types of risk-taking behaviors required for genuine cognitive growth to occur. Without taking cognitive risks, students limit their learning potential.

We teach reading and writing at all grade levels from kindergarten through high school. We challenge students to use their minds to solve problems, create stories, and respond to issues and ideas that they've never before encountered. We encourage our students to think critically and generate hypotheses. Behind all successful students is a belief that they can and will succeed at the academic challenges that teachers present to them. But what about those students who don't do particularly well at reading the first two years of formal schooling? What about the students who never develop effective writing strategies? What about students who have been persuaded by their teachers that mathematics is not their strong suit? Many of these students never develop or use the necessary risk-taking behaviors required for substantial cognitive growth.

Among the characteristics of "good" thinkers is risk taking (Glatthorn and Baron 1991). Risk taking is also a characteristic of effective readers and writers at the elementary school level (May 1998). Taking risks is a joy to many of us, but for the students who seldom are recognized for academic success, taking a risk, such as reading out loud to the other students in class, is viewed as a losing prospect. Students who meet with minimal success in school because of academic difficulty, learning disabilities, or behavioral problems ask the same question daily: "Why play a game that I will never win?" To protect themselves, these students refuse to participate, out of fear that they will never receive recognition for their efforts, only for their products. Their schoolwork may never meet the unrealistic standards often developed by state legislators, local school boards, or their own teachers. These frustrations create a constant feeling of inadequacy.

No adult would be foolish enough to participate in a losing effort for 180 days a year for thirteen consecutive years; yet we expect struggling students to return to school year after year despite their inability to succeed. Let's face it, if you don't believe that you can succeed at something, why would you continue to try—only to fail over and over again? For example, perhaps you don't play tennis well. Every time you play, you become frustrated by your lack of success in hitting the ball, placing it in the "right" place on the other side of the net, and your failure to win a game. Imagine your horror if every day a yellow bus came into your neighborhood and took you to the tennis courts for another day of failure! Yet every day, thousands of students get on the bus and head for school knowing that they will not succeed at many of the tasks they are asked to undertake.

In protecting themselves, some young adolescents refuse to take the very risks that are necessary to support future cognitive growth. Without the confidence, encouragement, or support to attempt new reading strategies, writing experiences, or learn new mathematical principles, many students wander aimlessly through school without furthering their education for fear of looking like a fool. Many children begin to believe that they will never succeed as students even before they reach young adolescence. These students are quite capable of learning, but their learning doesn't involve academics and seldom occurs at school!

Teachers have the responsibility to reach out to these students. Professional educators are hired to meet the needs of all students—not merely the gifted and talented ones. Meeting cognitive needs is secondary to meeting students' needs for a safe learning environment that encourages them to take risks.

For students, academic safety means that

- no one laughs at them when they attempt to ask or answer a question
- teachers establish realistic academic expectations and outcomes for each student
- students' efforts are recognized as well as the products of those efforts
- teachers eliminate competitive situations that create inequity among students
- teachers develop cooperative grouping strategies that encourage students to collaborate in their learning and share their knowledge and expertise with one another
- teachers play the role of learning facilitator to encourage student independence
- teachers choose alternative instructional strategies to meet each student's learning style
- teachers recognize and appreciate talents other than academic skills.

We understand that providing this type of attention to each student may seem impossible. If you're not sure you are up to meeting the challenge, ask this question of yourself: "If schooling were not mandatory, how would my behavior as an educator encourage each student to return to my class every day?" Answering this question requires serious reflection. You affect many young lives as a teacher. Interacting positively with your students is imperative.

Recognizing and Responding to Diverse Learners

If you care about young adolescents and their need to learn, you will spend much of the first few weeks of the school year studying how each student operates in a classroom environment. After discovering what works well for each student, you will provide the conditions needed for his or her learning and the tools each student will need to succeed at new cognitive challenges. A most important characteristic of becoming an effective, caring educator is the ability and commitment to recognize individual learning differences among students.

Ineffective teachers use the same materials, lesson plans, and testing practices with every student year after year, disregarding individual learning needs. Effective educators ask the question, "What is it that I can do to help each student to successfully learn this year?" Effective teachers design classroom learning experiences that match the needs of all students: those with different ethnic backgrounds, those with special learning disabilities, those from low socioeconomic neighborhoods, and students who excel in all academic areas.

Although much has been written about strategies for teaching diverse and at-risk student populations, we adopt the view that a responsive middle level teacher takes all students' characteristics into consideration when planning and delivering instruction and assessing students. Effective teachers who recognize and react to diverse learners are extremely flexible in the ways that they present information to students, allow students to complete assignments, and design assessment of students' learning. In the typical classroom with a range of diverse learners, student learning may be facilitated by the teacher in many different ways. Each student develops a separate set of expectations and outcomes based on his or her needs. We believe that committed, caring teachers make an effort to discover the strengths and weaknesses of their students and adjust their teaching to meet individual needs.

Sharing Decision Making

We are frequently confused by the beliefs that preservice and inservice teachers have about their roles as teachers. We hear that teachers must "take control," "discipline students," and make sure that students don't "get out of line." Many teachers view their role as that of an authority figure, unilaterally responsible for making the rules, enforcing them, and revising them on an ad hoc basis. We live in a country founded on democratic principles. Teachers can be instrumental in helping young adolescents develop democratic ideals when students are permitted to influence the policies and procedures used to govern their behavior.

We suspect that the fear associated with the idea of a democratic classroom is based on adult skepticism that young people are capable of making appropriate decisions about their education. Educators who share this mistrust of students fail to recognize that classrooms designed to provide opportunities for student choice are much more meaningful learning environments than those in which all decisions are made by the teacher.

Now, you might be asking yourself, "Where is the middle ground? How do I create a classroom in which students participate in the learning process without infringing on my authority?" The next question you might ask is, "How do I perform in the role of teacher if I relinquish control over how the classroom is organized or what the rules are?" Remember that young adolescents are curious about the existing authoritative system. They are beginning to question the rules, the policies, and the system of authority that they have subordinated themselves to unthinkingly for so long. It is an exciting and, to some, a threatening thought that students are beginning to dismantle the entire moral, behavioral framework that others have built up around them. They are chipping away at previously accepted rules, finding serious flaws in their structure. What an excellent time for teachers to engage students in dialogue on topics such as civic order, the reason for authority, self-management of behavior, accepting responsibility, and appropriate and reasonable decision making.

Teachers don't need to do the work of establishing class rules and policies by themselves—why waste the growing cognitive powers of young adolescents? Now is the time to have students participate in designing the classroom atmosphere. Initiate discussions on the role of students and teachers in creating an effective and dynamic learning environment. Use class meetings to decide how to appropriately handle violations of trust and foster respect among students and between students and teachers.

Shared decision making lays the foundation for a classroom that operates as a community. When students view their classmates as partners in a joint venture, involved in a process of learning from one an-other, the classroom becomes a place of communal cognitive process-ing, where each individual's contributions are valued.

Student Involvement in Curricular Decision Making

Inviting students to collaborate with teachers on curriculum develop-ment marks a radical departure from traditional schooling practices. After all, many educators question whether *teachers* should participate in curricular decision-making, let alone students! But schools must be-come places in which the information that students learn has meaning for them. Curricular outcomes designed without the voices of middle school students are likely to have little impact on influencing the lives of young adolescents. As stated in the National Middle School Asso-ciation's *This We Believe* (1995), "Consonant with their varying capac-ities to handle responsibility, students must be nurtured in making choices and decisions about curricular goals, content, methodology, activities, materials, and means of assessment" (22).

How relevant to their lives will their class work be if textbook writ-ers, curriculum supervisors, or teachers make unilateral decisions about content intended for the young adolescent? The curriculum is mean-ingful only if it responds to the personal questions and concerns that students have. Strategies for involving students in curricular planning are discussed in Chapter 5.

Creating Collaborative—Not Competitive—
Learning Environments

One of the most disturbing aspects of the traditional school experience is the pitting of children against one another in academic endeavors. Young adolescents clearly understand how diverse their academic abil-ities are. Teachers who create competitive learning situations accen-tuate the weaknesses and strengths of students. The public comparison is embarrassing for less able students. As a result, they refuse to take the risks necessary for learning to occur. If being "the best" is what suc-cess means—and that is the idea in many schools—most students will fail at school. Kohn (1986) states that a competitive learning environment, "distracts you from a task at a given moment; makes you less interested in that task over the long run, and this results in poorer performance" (60–61). Contrary to what you may have been led to believe, competitive environments do not result in increased learning.

Students in collaborative classrooms work together to solve problems, plan presentations, design projects, develop questions, and resolve personal differences. Kohn (1986) explains that "a cooperative classroom is not simply one where students sit together or talk with each other or even share materials. It means that successful completion of a task depends on each student and therefore each has an incentive to want the other(s) to succeed" (6).

Collaboration among students doesn't automatically occur when teachers ask students to work together. The teacher's role is to plan instructional activities that encourage student cooperation and to assist students in developing the social strategies needed to successfully work together. Following group work sessions, middle level students should be asked to evaluate their collaborative efforts to determine how to improve their skills in this area. Students may rate their skills as team members in categories such as

- effectiveness in listening to one another
- ability to accept various individual responsibilities
- willingness to alter original beliefs to reach consensus
- ability to establish and meet deadlines

Your students will be able to work independently in group activities after a few evaluative sessions of their teamwork.

In this chapter, we have provided a number of suggestions for teachers looking to positively influence student learning. Educators must question traditional practices that foster hostile learning environments. Most of us experienced these ourselves in our own time as students. You can change such negative conditions to create a more positive learning environment. Students, like plants, grow well when they are cultivated with care. The more comfortable and secure your students feel when they are with you each day, the more growth they will experience.

We have asked you to examine your personal beliefs about the treatment of students, and how your behaviors can genuinely affect the creation of a positive learning community. As you continue to develop your philosophical beliefs on these issues, our discussion of effective middle schools continues in the next chapter as we examine how to structure curriculum so that students own their learning.

Time for Reflection

- Based on your reading to this point, add to the list of effective teacher characteristics that you developed at the beginning of this chapter.
- Review your list with a classmate who has written one, and compare the similarities and differences.
- How do you think the role of teachers has changed since you were a middle school student? How have teacher roles remained the same?
- Discuss with your classmates your views on the importance of using class time to develop a learning community.

References

BARTH, R. S. 1991. *Improving Schools from Within.* San Francisco: Jossey-Bass.

BOSWORTH, K. 1995. "Caring for Others and Being Cared For: Students Talk About Caring in School." *Phi Delta Kappan* 76, no. 9: 686–693.

BRENDTRO, L. M., M. BROKENLEG, AND S. VAN BOCKERN. 1990. *Reclaiming Youth at Risk: Our Hope for the Future.* Bloomington, IN: National Education Service.

CAINE, R. N., and G. CAINE. 1994. *Making Connections: Teaching and the Human Brain.* Menlo Park, CA: Addison Wesley.

CHARNEY, R. S. 1991. *Teaching Children to Care.* Pittsfield, MA: Northeast Foundation for Children.

CHASKIN, R. J., AND D. MENDLEY RAUNER. 1995. "Youth and Caring." *Phi Delta Kappan* 76, no. 9: 667–674.

ELIAS, M. J., J. E. ZINS, R. P. WEISSBERG, K. S. FREY, M. T. GREENBERG, N. M. HAYNES, R. KESSLER, M. E. SCHWAB-STONE, AND T. P. SHRIVER. 1997. *Promoting Social and Emotional Learning: Guidelines for Educators.* Alexandria, VA: Association for Supervision and Curriculum Development.

GLATTHORN, A. A., AND J. BARON. 1991. "The Good Thinker." In *Developing Minds: A Resource Book for Teaching Thinking.* ed. A. L. Costa. Rev. ed., Alexandria, VA: Association for Supervision and Curriculum Development, 63–67.

GOODMAN, J. F., V. SUTTON, AND I. HARKEVY. 1995. "The Effectiveness of Family Workshops in a Middle School Setting: Respect and Caring Make a Difference." *Phi Delta Kappan* 76, no. 9: 694–700.

KAGAN, S. 1994. *Cooperative Learning.* San Juan Capistrano, CA: Kagan Cooperative Learning.

KOHN, A. 1986. *No Contest: The Case Against Competition, Why We Lose in Our Race to Win.* Boston: Houghton Mifflin.

LIPSITZ, J. 1995. "Prologue: Why We Should Care About Caring." *Phi Delta Kappan* 76, no. 9: 665–666.

MAY, F. B. 1998. *Reading as Communication: To Help Children Write and Read.* 5th ed. Upper Saddle River, NJ: Merrill Prentice Hall.

NATIONAL MIDDLE SCHOOL ASSOCIATION. 1995. *This We Believe: Developmentally Responsive Middle Level Schools.* 3rd ed. Columbus, OH: National Middle School Association.

PERRY, B. D. 1996. *Maltreated Children: Experience, Brain Development, and the Next Generation.* New York: Norton.

FIVE

Student Designed Curriculum

*I think the curriculum should change. There are teachers
that I have who photocopy the same sheet for ten years,
the same worksheet, every year the same thing. Like
Germany, the teacher said, "Write East and West
Germany." I would make teachers have to change their
curriculum. Every year they would have to modify it.*

EIGHTH-GRADE STUDENT

While many positive changes have been
made in the education of young adolescents,
most schools have not tackled the hard and
often political question of the middle school
curriculum. Teachers have changed *how*
they teach but in many cases they have not
changed *what* they teach. Educational content is often the same from middle school to
middle school; it looks surprisingly like that
of the junior high school, which looks sur-
prisingly like that of the high school, which
looks surprisingly like that of schools fifty to seventy-five years ago—
despite dramatic changes in the way *life* looks today. As Sue Swaim,
executive director of the NMSA, said in 1993, "While a continually
increasing number of schools have moved to implement interdisciplinary teams, teacher advisor programs, broad exploratory experiences,

skill development programs, and other recommended characteristics, the basic questions of what we teach and how we teach remain for the most part, unanswered and little challenged" (xii).

Most middle schools do not design their curriculum based on an understanding of young adolescent development. This chapter analyzes what a developmentally appropriate middle school curriculum should be. This chapter precedes our discussions of instruction and school structure because we believe that curriculum should be the central focus of any middle school. If a school has implemented changes in school structure, the school day, and modes of instruction, but has not changed the curriculum to respond to developmental issues, it can not meet the needs of young adolescents.

Time for Reflection
- What qualities make a job satisfying to you?
- Why are chores (laundry, house cleaning) sometimes so frustrating?
- Why do so many students look forward to ending their formal education even though that might mean facing the world of work (perhaps menial work) and having a standard of living lower than when their parents supported them?

CLARK (1997)

Look at how you answered the above questions. Now think of schooling at the middle level. According to the criteria you devised in answering the first question, would middle school be satisfying? Does it have any of the characteristics of a task that is frustrating? What is it about school that makes so many students want to get out? If middle level students had a choice, would they sign up for the teachers that they were assigned to? Would they voluntarily sign up to be in your class? Why is achievement so important in our lives and how can that translate to middle level education?

What Is Curriculum?

Before we look at what the curriculum of the middle school should be, let's clarify terms. Curriculum *is not:*

- a collection of textbooks or guides
- a fixed course of study
- that which the teacher prefers to teach
- a program of study that must be completed before the end of the school year

Curriculum *is:*

- the total experience of students at school
- a plan that involves students in learning
- a construct that enables students to access, process, interpret, and make connections to information
- the organizing focus of a school

Curriculum permeates the life of adolescents in school; they are immersed in it. It is what happens to them from the moment they walk into the building until they leave at the end of the day. It includes social times, club times, athletics, lunch, after-school programs, drama, music—every planned and unplanned event. Curriculum is every event that occurs in the life of students from the time they enter the building until they leave.

Beliefs About Middle Level Curriculum

Early Thinking

The discussion about curriculum is not new. When Donald Eichhorn first engaged in middle level reform in Upper St. Clair, Pennsylvania, not only did he revamp the organization and structure of the junior high school, he also challenged common assumptions about what should be taught and how best to teach it. He believed that the focus on curricular change would ultimately define what middle level education was all about. As Eichhorn stated in 1967, "The middle school concept, founded in the dramatic developments in human growth and development as well as in the society in which youngsters interact, may emerge into a successful organizational pattern, but only if educators develop programs commensurate with the characteristics of the ten to thirteen year old in all respects" (51).

Eichhorn was not alone in his beliefs about curriculum. In 1969 Conrad Toepfer, another early advocate of middle level education, commented, "It is not difficult to find junior high school administrators who conclude that all that needs be done to achieve the unfulfilled objectives of the junior high school is to replace it with a middle school organization, add water, and stir. The only predictable result of such a nostrum would seem to be a continued lack of definitive curricular programs for early adolescents!" (135).

Early philosophical discussions emphasized the need to design programs that focused on personal growth and would help students develop the responsibility and skills to interact with their world (David 1998; Dickinson 1993). These discussions were only moderately successful in impacting young adolescent education. The middle school curriculum still looks essentially like the high school's.

Current Discussions

Conversations among scholars on appropriate middle level curriculum models continue. Authors representing the NMSA, in its position paper *This We Believe*, (1995) wrote, "To most, curriculum refers to the content and skills to be covered in courses. In developmentally responsive middle level schools, however, curriculum embraces every planned aspect of a school's educational program" (20). The middle school curriculum must touch on those issues that concern young adolescents and help them construct meaning about themselves, their world, and their future. Thus defined, NMSA advocates a middle school curriculum that is "challenging, integrative and exploratory" (20) to best meet the needs of young adolescents.

Challenging

A challenging curriculum provides students with the opportunity to explore significant issues in their lives as they attempt to understand themselves and the world around them. Students become actively engaged in the learning process as they address relevant problems. They are empowered to use their knowledge and skills in significant ways and assume control over their own learning.

Absurd

A million miles from nowhere
Sitting alone in my chair
Listening to them whine
A straight line
Is the best way to lose your mind
Doing paper after paper
Where is the laughter
or the learning
It's disturbing
Rote, Rote, Rote
Whipped at our backs
Age old attacks,
It's a fact.
Change to them
is a four letter word
It's so damn absurd.

RICHARD BORDEAUX (1992)

Integrative

"Curriculum is integrative when it helps students make sense out of their life experiences" (NMSA 1995, 22). Curriculum areas are related in ways that help students find answers to their questions. In addition, the skills needed to solve problems are incorporated into the learning process. What happens in the classroom is connected to the students' lives and to the world outside of the school. Effective curriculum design also integrates issues of diversity and democracy; the multiple perspectives of all students are valued, validated, and explored.

Exploratory
Young adolescents are intensely curious about themselves and the world around them. Their expanding thinking capabilities open their minds to endless possibilities. Middle school should be a time when they can explore these possibilities. A curriculum rich in opportunities can help early adolescents discover things about themselves as they look at ways to make contributions to society. New forms of knowledge and new ways of looking at ideas can become lifetime pursuits. Students who have never had the opportunity to explore photography, quilting, world languages, kayaking, Internet surfing, hiking, astronomy, and a myriad of other areas can do so, broadening their conceptions of themselves and their world.

Basic Approaches to Curriculum Organization

How can a middle school provide a curriculum that is challenging, integrative, and exploratory? Does a traditional view of the curriculum embrace these qualities? To help us answer those questions as well as the difficult question of what the curriculum should be for middle level students, we will first explore the ways that curriculum can be organized and analyze the benefits and weaknesses in each organizational method. There are two basic ways to organize curriculum: through a subject-centered, discipline-based approach or through curriculum integration.

Subject-Centered, Discipline-Based Approach

Standard Fare—Subject-Oriented Curriculum
Most middle schools organize their curriculum around discrete subjects. In this approach, middle school teachers assume roles similar to their high school colleagues. The teachers are specialists in a specific curriculum area and their responsibility is to teach the students the knowledge and skills that their subject area requires.

In a middle school, subject-specific teaching is often implemented through the formation of a team of teachers, with each teacher responsible for a specific discipline. Usually the team consists of a math, science, social studies, and language arts teacher. Two-person teams are used in some schools. One teacher might be responsible for social studies and language arts while the other handles science and mathematics.

In the purest sense of this approach, the teachers, although a team, are concerned about covering their subject material and do not integrate knowledge across subject areas. Each teacher follows some designated curriculum or textbook and chooses those topics that are "mandated" by the district, appear in the textbook, or are personal areas of interest. The single-discipline approach to the curriculum tends to be textbook driven and teacher led.

Look at the results. Eighth graders arrive at school. In science class they learn about the structure of the atom. In social studies they study Brazil and the Amazon Valley. On to language arts, where students analyze plot and character development in the novel *The Westing Game* (Raskin 1978). Mathematics is the next subject. Half of the students go to eighth grade math, where they work on interest rates and percentages. The other half go to algebra to learn how to solve complex equations. Does this approach make sense for young adolescents? Is a curriculum thus designed challenging, integrative, and exploratory?

The subject approach does have its benefits. Most teachers have been trained as subject-area specialists. They are confident about their knowledge base and their ability to teach what they know best. Teachers are successful in planning and implementing lessons in their area of expertise.

Planning using the subject approach takes less time than attempting to integrate subject matter with other teachers on the team. Planning time is a precious commodity to teachers. Any type of team teaching requires collaboration, which necessitates common planning times.

Some teachers and administrators argue for a subject approach based on state and local curricular mandates as well as required standardized tests. The argument goes that if we don't teach specific items, students will score low on the achievement tests, which will reflect badly on students, teachers, and administrators. Furthermore, some educators argue that the structure of the high school mandates that single subjects be taught, each focusing on specific content knowledge.

The concerns about high school requirements, college entrance, state and local mandates, and achievement tests also encourage parents to support the subject approach. Parents wonder, "Will my child do well on the SAT? Will he/she have the knowledge needed for high school?" Breaking middle school curricular traditions is difficult for parents to understand.

In 1990, a book was published by the NMSA that questioned the traditional ways of thinking about curriculum. In *A Middle School Curriculum: From Rhetoric to Reality*, James Beane (1993) challenged the separate subject approach:

> Life and learning consist of a continuous flow of experiences around situations that require problem-solving in both large and small ways. When we encounter life situations or problems we do not ask, "which part is science, which is mathematics, which is history, and so on?" Rather we use whatever information or skills the situation itself calls for and we integrate these in problem-solving. Certainly such information and skills may often be found within subject areas, but in real life the problem itself is at the center and the information and skills are defined around the problem. In other words, the subject approach is alien to life itself. Put simply, it is "bad" learning theory. (45)

When a curriculum is implemented with few links between subject areas, students have difficulty making connections between what they are learning in school and the significant issues that impact their lives. At a time in development when cognitive processes are expanding and the world is filled with endless possibilities, will textbook-driven topics best help young adolescents understand their world and make sense of who they are? In a world that may appear contradictory and confusing, a curriculum that is textbook driven and reflects little student input does not offer the challenging and integrative curriculum that best engages them in learning. Textbooks rarely provide for exploration or offer connections, often propagate the status quo, and typically present information from a white, male European point of view. The relevance that students crave, the challenge that they demand, and the connections that they require are difficult to find in such a curriculum.

We are not saying that the acquisition of content is developmentally inappropriate for middle level students. We are saying that we must look at the content and ask how it contributes to helping students explore the significant issues in their lives. What knowledge is important? What knowledge is valued? For this age, how should we use knowledge? The fragmented, disjointed approach of a subject-centered curriculum makes it difficult to find continuity in learning. Although you may use instructional techniques that make your subject enjoyable, you still must ask whether a curriculum thus conceived is the most appropriate.

When we look at the developing social, physical, emotional, and cognitive needs of the young adolescent we begin to understand that what young adolescents need is a curriculum that engages them intellectually. They need a curriculum that provides opportunities for wide exploration, encourages interactions with the broader social world, helps them see connections between content knowledge and life, teaches them democratic ideals, and provides active hands-on exploration. All this activity must occur within a context of learning the skills needed to function in society, now and in the future. In many ways, the single subject approach fails to meet the developmental needs of the young adolescent.

Multidisciplinary Approach—Still Subject Specific
Theme teaching has become popular in many middle schools. In a multidisciplinary curriculum, teachers choose themes that can be correlated across two or more subject areas. The teams then determine what it is that each subject and each teacher can contribute to the theme. The simplest form of multidisciplinary planning is called "parallel teaching." In this approach, two or more teachers analyze their curricula for the year to see if there are common topics to cover and plan to teach these topics simultaneously. For example, when the history teacher covers the Revolutionary War, students read *Johnny Tremain* (Forbes 1944) in language arts class. As students study World War II in history class, they read *The Diary of a Young Girl* (Frank 1967) in language arts. While students explore the geology of Massachusetts in

science class, they study the history of the state in social studies. Although teachers are focusing on a similar topic, no overall goals and objectives are common in the two classes.

A more complex form of multidisciplinary teaching involves the entire team in planning. A common theme or topic is chosen after considering state or local curricular frameworks, textbooks, or teacher interests. Once a topic is chosen, the teachers engage in discussions about what their specific subject area can offer to the study of that topic. They develop overall guiding questions, identify objectives, plan activities, and devise a final assessment project.

You'll notice in Figure 5.1 that once a theme is chosen, each teacher develops the activities and skills relevant to the content in their subject area. Little actual integration of subject areas occurs. Let's discuss a specific example. A team of teachers has chosen to do a unit on the Olympics. It's an Olympic year and they think that the students will be

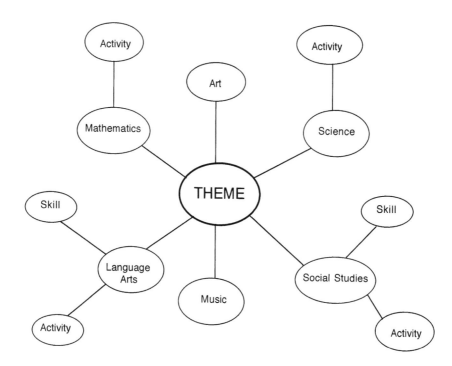

Figure 5.1   Thematic Planning—Multidisciplinary Approach

excited about the topic. The social studies teacher focuses on the history of the Olympic games from ancient Greece through the modern games (after all, ancient Greece is part of the seventh-grade curriculum). The teacher discusses how the Olympics have fared during wartimes. Students study world geography. They watch video clips of the parade of nations and investigate why Greece is always first in the parade and why the United States delegation never lowers its flag to the leaders of the host country. Students research countries that have been banned from the Olympics.

The science teacher talks about human anatomy, health and fitness, conditioning, and nutrition. Students analyze video clips of Olympic competitions. They investigate banned drugs and debate the use of drugs to enhance performance and whether rights are being violated with mandatory drug testing (a valid connection to a civics lesson for the social studies teacher). An innovative science teacher might have students research poles used in pole vaults, aluminum versus wooden bats in baseball, why people are running faster now, why changes in tennis rackets have changed the game, the physics of the curve ball, and so on.

In art they'll construct flags for a parade of nations. In music they'll learn the national anthems from different countries. In mathematics, they'll analyze distance, time, rate, height, weight, speed, percentages, runs batted in (RBIs), earned run averages (ERAs), and whatever other statistics they can think of. In language arts they'll read biographies, autobiographies, and novels about former and current Olympians as well as Greek mythology. They will reenact the first Olympiad. And of course the culminating experience will be in physical education class in which a mini-Olympics will be conducted.

This type of multidisciplinary teaching is common in middle schools. The teachers choose the topic, yet, despite the connections made between the subject areas, topics remain subject bound. The day is still divided into social studies, mathematics, science, language arts, and reading. Sometimes longer blocks of time are devoted to certain activities, but subject areas remain intact. Content is taught because it helps teach the concepts and principles predetermined by teachers.

There are many benefits to a multidisciplinary approach. Such units meet the needs of the young adolescent in a way that discrete subject teaching is unable to do. Students are able to see connections between subject areas. They learn not only content but also how to apply content learned in one area to another.

Affective benefits are just as important. The units can be fun. A sense of team spirit permeates the school day. All the teachers know what's going on in every class. They can talk with the students about their projects for other teachers. Multidisciplinary team teaching assures the students that their teachers are talking to one another.

One drawback of multidisciplinary planning, of course, is limited time for collaborative planning. When teams have little common planning time, the organization and implementation of thematic units is difficult. Activities can become disjointed.

A serious drawback is the tendency to make artificial and contrived connections between subject areas. Sometimes it is difficult to see how a specific subject area fits into a theme. For example, how do you relate mathematics to a study of the rain forest—do you graph all the different kinds of frogs? Thematic units lose their power if there are not clear and meaningful connections made between subject areas and the topics.

Even more problematic is the tendency to focus on popular and fun rather than significant and relevant themes. We recognize that the unit on the Olympics was fun, but did it provide significant knowledge? Was it, in fact, challenging, integrative, and exploratory? Was it truly meaningful for young adolescents? Did it help students understand themselves and the world around them? Did it challenge them to explore their world? Was it the best way to spend student time?

Interdisciplinary Approach

Does the multidisciplinary approach extend deep enough to meet the needs of young adolescents? While topics such as the Olympics may engage and excite students, something is lacking: the connection to the real concerns and questions that middle school students have about themselves and the world around them.

In an attempt to better meet the needs of middle level students, some teams choose themes not based on the textbook or teacher interests but on what they think would be meaningful to the students. Since many students have a heightened awareness of their natural surroundings at this time, a team may choose the environment as a theme. Questions to be answered include: What are some of the causes of pollution? What effect does air pollution have on the human body? What can we do to minimize their ill effects? As teacher teams look at the questions, each teacher decides where he or she can best facilitate learning and develops activities accordingly. Although teachers may still ask what their subject area can provide to the study of the theme, more attempts are made to integrate knowledge in meaningful ways. Rather than simply being multidisciplinary with teachers focusing on what their subject has to offer, teaching in this model becomes more interdisciplinary, with some of the boundaries between subject areas beginning to dissolve. The social studies teacher might talk about the historical implications of scientific research in the rain forest. Together the science and social studies teachers plan long blocks of time where students engage in scientific and historical inquiry. On other days, the science and mathematics teachers might have extended blocks of time to analyze the data created from students' questions.

Interdisciplinary differs from multidisciplinary teaching in two significant ways. First, to develop themes, teachers consider what interests the students have. Second, the boundaries between subjects begin to blur as teachers combine subject areas in order to explore principles.

In the interdisciplinary approach, themes and activities are still primarily chosen by the teacher. Teachers haven't asked students what is significant in their lives. Although the interdisciplinary model provides more opportunities for middle school students to engage in challenging meaningful learning, is it engaging enough for young adolescents? Can we, in fact, go even further and organize the curriculum around the questions and concerns of the young adolescent and not around textbooks, mandates, or the interests of separate subject teachers? Can we design a curriculum that not only focuses on significant knowledge and teaches the skills to use that knowledge, but also infuses classrooms with the important issues of democracy and diversity? If so, how?

Curriculum Integration Model: A Different Way of Thinking About the Curriculum

---

Time for Reflection

In Chapter 1 you were asked what you thought was the most important thing a middle school student could do or learn at school.

- How did you respond then?
- Is your answer the same now?
- What experiences have influenced your response?

Here's what a group of middle school students said when they were asked about the most important thing to learn in school:

> I think the most important thing to learn is how to live in the real world. . . . We need to learn stuff about life and looking ahead.
>
> EIGHTH GRADER

> I don't think about what job I'm going to get in the future. I think more about what morals I've learned. I think I should first develop a group of morals that I think are right and then I can deal with what job I do later or what I want to learn.
>
> GRACE, SEVENTH GRADER

> I don't think that when we grow up anybody will come up on the street and say, 'Excuse me, do you know who Constantine was?' We're learning about Constantine and his son and his son's son and his son's cousin. They didn't do anything in history but we learned about it.
>
> JASON, SEVENTH GRADER

> The most important thing to learn is to be responsible.
>
> EIGHTH GRADER

If we are to have a curriculum that makes sense for the young adolescent, it must be one that responds to their concerns about the world, to those issues that they feel are important. A curriculum organization based on the curriculum integration model attempts to do just that—to design the curriculum around the lives of young adolescents. In such a model, the curriculum is developed collaboratively by teachers and students and arises from the questions and concerns of the students rather than the demands of the subject areas. Teachers who adopt this model ask questions about sources of knowledge and how that knowledge can and should be used within the context of young adolescent lives. Subject area knowledge becomes vital as it helps students answer their questions or solve their problems. The key, however, is that the organizing factor does not focus on the subject areas but rather on student questions and concerns. According to Beane (1997): "Curriculum integration is a curriculum design that is concerned with enhancing the possibilities for personal and social integration through the organization of curriculum around significant problems and issues, collaboratively identified by educators and young people, without regard for subject-area boundaries" (x–xi).

Early adolescents are intensely curious about their world and their ultimate place in that world. They are developing their own values and learning what it means to have ethical relationships in an often confusing social climate. Given these developmental issues, it makes sense to devise a curriculum that puts them and their concerns at the center. How does the curriculum integration model achieve that?

In *A Middle School Curriculum: From Rhetoric to Reality* (1993), Beane questioned the existing curriculum design of most middle schools. Drawing on the work of the progressive movement in the early part of the twentieth century, he advocated developing a curriculum that has meaning to early adolescents by focusing on their lives to design themes for study. Beane presented eight guidelines for the middle school curriculum. After analyzing these eight guidelines, we will explore how curriculum integration supports these guidelines and describe how to use that model in the classroom.

Beane's Guidelines for a Middle School Curriculum

1. "The middle school curriculum should focus on general education" (Beane 1993, 17). All students should be exposed to a broad range of educational experiences. Middle school is not the time to sift, sort, and select—to put some students in honors classes while others stay in remedial classes, to expose some to significant issues while providing memory games for other students. A general education focuses on the needs and concerns of all young people in society. We must provide learning opportunities that are accessible to all students and provide a successful common learning experience for all.

2. "The central purpose of the middle school curriculum should be helping early adolescents explore self and social meanings at this time in their lives" (18). Yes, we have state mandates as well as pressures from parents and society. Those concerns are secondary to meeting the needs of young adolescents. And, as we shall see, designing a curriculum that helps students explore their lives provides access to vast amounts of knowledge and acquisition of skills to adequately process and use that knowledge.

3. "The middle school curriculum should respect the dignity of early adolescents" (18). Young adolescents are not just hormones with feet, nor are they empty-headed teens concerned about nothing. Middle school students are dynamic young people who have deep concerns about life and the survival of the world. Their struggles to achieve independence and demonstrate responsibility are genuine. Their faith in their ability to solve problems is immense. The curriculum should be designed to take advantage of these concerns and the energy with which students will tackle them. Our faith in students should encourage faith in themselves.

4. "The middle school curriculum should be firmly grounded in democracy" (19). One of the goals of the school system is to provide students with opportunities to explore the democratic way of life. Yet, the school environment seldom offers the

opportunity to practice democracy. More often than not our schools are run as an autocracy where one person possesses unlimited power over others rather than as a democracy. What is learned, how it is taught and the consequences of behavior are in the hands of that one person.

As Amanda, an eighth grader, put it, "I think students should have more rule over the school. A lot of teachers will say, 'This isn't a democracy' and they're putting us in a dictator's world in this school, and I don't like it at all."

Another eighth grader commented, "In middle school I feel like a robot. You go where you're assigned to go and do what you're told."

If we want students to be firmly grounded in the tenets upon which this country was founded, we must begin in the classroom, starting with the curriculum. Therefore, the curriculum must be democratically constructed through student-teacher collaboration. Control, power, and decision making must be shared.

5. "The middle school curriculum should honor diversity" (19). In an attempt to honor diversity in the classroom, teachers often expose students to diverse ways of thinking. After this exposure, however, students are told to complete the assigned projects in a timely fashion, following the guidelines and rubrics prepared by the teacher.

    Exposure to diverse ways of thinking isn't enough. Multiple viewpoints should be at the core of our curriculum, offering students diverse ways of analyzing and exploring problems and multiple ways of expressing viewpoints. Different ways of approaching knowledge should not only be valued but also validated. It is through this validation that students can create personal meaning out of knowledge.

6. "The middle school curriculum should be of great personal and social significance" (20). Although fun units can initially motivate students, teach skills, and expose students to new content, these units frequently lack the significance needed for real student learning. Fun units are often just that—fun.

Students need to study significant topics and themes that help them construct meaning out of their lives. They should explore the questions and concerns they have about themselves and the world around them. One eighth grader mentioned to us, "I think you should be able to pick what you're interested in to study. We don't get choices for most stuff."

7. "The middle school curriculum should be lifelike and lively" (20). "Class is so long and boring. Instead of doing fun things, you just read out of a book" (Tim, seventh grader). Middle school students are and want to be learners. The curriculum should embrace wonder, curiosity, exploration, problem solving, challenges, and action. Lifelike and lively does not mean fun, yet insignificant. Young adolescents are ready to use their minds—let's give them the chance to do so.

8. "The middle school curriculum should enhance knowledge and skills for all young people" (21). All students should have access to knowledge and develop the skills to use that knowledge to create a better world. Knowledge is a powerful tool for solving problems and answering questions. Knowledge is most powerful, however, when it is used on a quest for meaning. Skills become the tools to access, process, and use that knowledge.

Curriculum Integration in the Middle School Classroom

Curriculum that embraces a separate-subject approach makes it difficult to achieve these guidelines. Through curriculum integration, however, all students can access knowledge that has meaning and relevance to them. In this approach, students explore themes that emerge out of their personal and social concerns. Themes are chosen through a collaborative effort by teachers and students. After themes are chosen, teachers do not look at their separate discipline to determine what to study. Instead, students and teachers together determine what activities can be used to explore concepts, solve problems, or answer questions without regard to subject areas. Skills are embedded in the learning process as they become necessary prerequisites for engaging in activities or solving problems. But perhaps most importantly, as a result of collaboration, students are exposed to the enduring concepts of democracy, including human dignity and cultural diversity.

While you might agree with the philosophy of curriculum integration, it may be difficult to see how you can implement it in a classroom or team setting. To find themes that revolve around concerns that young adolescents have about themselves and the world around them, teachers must solicit student input. The next step is to identify the skills and develop the activities that will help students explore the issues, answer their questions, and solve their problems.

James Beane (1998) describes five steps as the most successful way of implementing curriculum integration. These steps may take a number of days to complete. The initial step involves student reflection. Beane suggests that teachers begin by providing opportunities for such reflection. Ask students to list words that describe who they are and what they like. Students might say things like, "I like horses." "I like going to Hawaii." "I am a swimmer, and I like to play baseball." "In my spare time I play street hockey and football." Because students have rarely been given the opportunity to have input into the development of the curriculum, they engage in the process more easily if they are first given the opportunity to individually reflect and to answer questions about who they are.

Students can be asked to choose the things on the list they like best about themselves and what they would like to change. They can think about what they would like to be like—what words they wish they had on their list. These lists can be kept private or shared in small or large groups.

After students have had time to reflect, the second step of the process is to ask students two questions. The first is, "What questions and concerns do you have about yourself?" After individually answering that question, students get into small groups to share their questions, search for common questions, and combine similar ideas in order to generate a group list. Each group presents its list to the class. The key to success is to validate the questions and concerns of all students. Everything gets put on the list during this initial session.

One group of seventh and eighth graders listed the following questions:

- How do you get people to like you?
- How about dating?
- What's wrong with public displays of affection?
- Why do I have to have hair on my legs?
- Why do we have to impress to fit in?
- Why are you judged on appearance (hair, skin color, clothes, jewelry)?
- What will I be when I grow up?
- How do we get money, and how much is enough?
- Why do we alter our looks (hair, plastic surgery, tattoos, piercings)?
- What is your uvula for?
- Why do bones break?
- Why can't you wear hats and coats in schools?
- Why can't you have skateboards in school?
- Why are the lockers so small in the locker room?
- Why do I have to take gym and health?
- Why do you have to take the things you have to take?
- How does high school work—schedules, work, popularity?
- Where will I live?
- Will I be wealthy?
- Will I ever look good?
- Will I ever stop fighting with my sister?
- Will I be successful in life?
- What college will I go to?
- Will I be in peace or in danger?

The second question moves from the personal to a broader category: "What questions and concerns do you have about the world?" Once they have listed, analyzed, and combined the questions they have about themselves, students engage in a similar process with the questions and concerns they have about the world around them—school, family, community, city, nation, world. For example:

- How about the environment—why do we destroy it instead of saving it?
- Why is the world round?
- Why do we slaughter animals for food?
- Will we have World War III?
- Will we ever come in contact with aliens?
- Is cloning a good idea?
- How can scientific progress help the world?
- How do phones and televisions work?
- Why are kids more advanced on the computers than their parents?
- How about prejudice—why do we judge people based on looks or clothes?
- Why are crazy people and murderers that way?
- Why isn't there the perfect crime?
- Why do teachers yell? Why are some people teachers if they don't want to be?
- Will America be the same when I grow up?
- How do diseases start? When will they come out with a cure for AIDS?
- Why do teenagers do drugs?
- Why do adults do drugs in front of teenagers?
- Why are there so many religions and opinions of religions?
- Why do we have gangs?
- Why do we have the death penalty?
- Why do we have war?
- Will the earth die?
- Why does the government cover up things?
- What is the soul? Is there an afterlife?
- Why do sports players make more money than teachers?
- Why is the color of a flame what it is?
- Why do all M&Ms taste the same and why do some people think they don't?
- How do they get the carbon dioxide in soda?
- How do you read a bar code?

This process takes time. Students whose genuine questions are frequently ignored may begin asking questions we think are superficial such as, "Why do locker rooms smell?" or "Why are coins round?" In fact, these questions are not superficial at all, but reflect the curiosity that is part of the young adolescent's life. These questions may later lead to a wonderful unit on "The Mysteries of the World."

Given the validity and respect for all questions, students will begin to list ideas that are of deeper concern to them: "Why do people have to judge you by the way you look rather than by what is inside?" "I'm concerned about the future of cloning, and what it will do to the wonderful diversity that we have today." "Why do we have gangs, and what can we do about all that hatred?"

Once students have listed their individual questions about the world, they again share with a small group and search for similar questions and ideas. Each group makes a list of the questions they have about the world that they share with the class.

The third step is for students to analyze both lists to look for connections between their personal and social concerns in order to develop some common themes. Students see that their questions about wearing hats and coats, taking classes they don't want to, teachers yelling, the government hiding things, gangs, crime, and the death penalty might all be related to the theme of *power*. They might look at their questions about technology, aliens, relationships, what job they'll have, high school, and cloning and come up with a common theme related to *the future*.

In the fourth step an initial theme must be chosen. Each group presents the common themes that they developed. These themes are posted and students try to develop consensus about what they want to study first. Sometimes this process involves identifying what themes were mentioned the most. Other times it might involve looking for correlations between themes and combining them. A decision might be reached by having groups choose their top three and bottom three themes and having students vote. Whatever the strategy, a theme is chosen, with the remaining topics reserved for later study.

Once a theme has been chosen, the final step is for students to go back to their original lists of questions and identify those that relate to the theme. They generate new questions, concerns, and problems related to the theme. They brainstorm the knowledge and skills needed to understand the theme well. Students suggest activities that will help them explore the concepts. If they choose the topic of *the future,* the students might have high school students come talk to the class. They might interview computer programmers, learn how to write résumés and fill out applications, or learn how to develop a family budget.

What is the teachers' role? First, the teacher must be a facilitator, helping students through the process of exploring their concerns and questions. Once a theme is chosen, teachers collaborate with students to develop activities to explore the themes. Each teacher on the team analyzes the activities and determines which ones they can best facilitate. Teachers expand and add to student ideas for activities, identify and collect resources, develop lessons related to the activities, create timelines, and integrate the skills students need to answer their questions. Chapter 6 will elaborate on the role of the teacher and student in the learning process. Notice in Figure 5.2 that the planning process

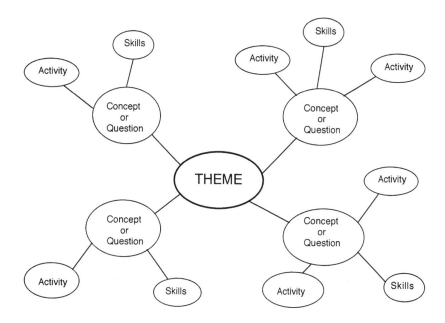

Figure 5.2   Curriculum Integration Model

focuses on the identification of significant concepts needed to explore the theme, rather than identifying how each content area contributes to the theme.

As you can see, the planning process for developing an integrated curriculum is radically different from the process used for developing multidisciplinary units. In curriculum integration, the process begins and is driven by the questions and concerns generated by students. Activities are chosen because they help students explore the concepts needed to answer the questions and concerns. Skills are taught because they are needed in order to solve problems inherent in the theme. Unlike the multidisciplinary curriculum, teachers do not adhere to specific subject-areas but use subject-area knowledge as needed. Content becomes vital and essential as students attempt to explore the significant issues they have raised.

Today curriculum integration has been implemented by teachers or teams in a few classrooms or schools; most schools continue to use traditional teaching models for curriculum. Two middle schools, Brown Barge School in Pensacola, Florida, and Carver Academy in Waco, Texas, have adopted curriculum integration as a model for the whole school (Powell 1999). The teachers in those schools do not teach specific subjects but instead guide students through specific units of study.

There are compelling reasons for implementing a curriculum integration model at the middle level. It is developmentally responsive; it allows for cognitive challenge, emotional self-exploration, social interaction, and physical movement; and it meets the diverse instructional needs of students and responds to issues of multiple intelligences, ethnic diversity, and students of differing abilities.

The more compelling reasons, however, relate to both the focus on real problems and concerns of the young adolescent and to issues of democracy in the classroom. A curriculum that focuses on the real concerns of the young adolescent leads to high motivation and significant learning. Collaborating with students demonstrates the values and morals inherent in the society in which we live. If we are to teach students the concepts of a democratic citizenship, we must model them in our classrooms. Collaboration between teachers and students gives ownership and power to all involved and respects the knowledge that everyone brings to the learning situation.

Students like it. Teachers like it.

Having a say is important. It prepares you for later in life when you have to speak out about future issues.

MOLLY, SEVENTH GRADE

Planning with students is the most challenging and most exciting thing I do.

SIXTH-GRADE TEACHER

I would probably quit education if I couldn't do this kind of work.

SEVENTH-GRADE TEACHER

There's nothing more important in the world than empowering students. It's exhausting.

SIXTH-GRADE TEACHER

I can't imagine doing it any other way.

SEVENTH- AND EIGHTH-GRADE TEACHER

Ultimately, middle level educators are going to have to ask what curriculum model is appropriate for young adolescents. If we could, in fact, design the perfect middle school, what would the curriculum look like? If we can envision a curriculum integration model as the most effective way to educate the young adolescent, why isn't it done that way? If curriculum integration is such a "perfect" and powerful model, why isn't it more widely used?

Grasping For Air
Four papers
Three worksheets
Too little time
I should have planned ahead
As time passed by
Tick
Tick
Tick
Where are my papers
and my pens
I better begin
Fore the day ends
Too much work
Too little time
Why
isn't quality
more important than quantity?
I know, because it's easier to change lead to gold
than a curriculum that's old.

RICHARD BORDEAUX

The reasons curriculum integration is not more widely used are many and varied. Teacher training, curriculum mandates, pressures from parents, dependence on textbooks, and a society that widely validates the traditional model lead most middle schools to stay with what has always been done.

Teacher attitudes and training are also important variables. The curriculum-integration model requires a shift in the way that teachers perceive their role in the classroom. The content areas that they have put so much effort into mastering become secondary, and at times insignificant, to their students' search for meaning. Suddenly teachers cannot fall back on what they have been trained to do. Planning is a challenge, as the learning process is dynamic and develops out of daily interaction with students. The uncertainty about what the day will hold can be unsettling when teachers no longer dictate the learning process.

Camille Barr, former principal at Brown Barge Middle School, described the difficulties of using the curriculum integration approach: "Integrative schooling is such hard work for teachers, much more demanding on their time and energy. And that's emerging as my biggest concern. Having the vision and creating and implementing it are one thing, but none of that compares to maintaining and sustaining it" (quoted in Powell 1999, 29).

Testing requirements and curriculum mandates are also important variables. Without a doubt, content is important. And without a doubt, a curriculum integration model provides content and conceptual understanding at a much deeper level than in a traditional curriculum. When a state education department, however, requires the teaching of ancient history in the seventh grade, many social studies teachers have a difficult time implementing a curriculum integration model. Teachers who believe in this model must continue to voice concerns about specific curriculum mandates and help educators, administrators, and legislators explore what curriculum is most appropriate for young adolescents and whether the middle level is the time to engage in content-specific teaching.

Parents create additional pressures. Because most parents grew up learning by means of a traditional curriculum, they feel comfortable with it. They worry about SAT scores, high school success, college entrance, and whether their child is learning what he or she needs to learn. Teachers often find themselves having to sell and defend their use of curriculum integration.

Stuck on a Team

Curriculum integration requires a philosophy of education that puts students, not subject areas, at the center. If a teacher finds himself or herself on a team with others who do not share this philosophy, it will be challenging to implement the curriculum integration model at a team level. What if you believe in the model but are stuck with a mandated curriculum?

Overcoming the obstacles may be difficult, but you can, in fact, do much in your own classroom to propagate the values of democracy and diversity through implementing a modified curriculum integration model. If your school is committed to the subject-area approach, you can still center your classroom curriculum around students' questions and concerns. You can then connect your subject-area teaching to broader understandings relevant to your students' lives.

Take students through the process of identifying questions about themselves and the world around them. Help them identify common themes that arise from these questions. Then, talk to students about the mandated curriculum. If, for example, your seventh graders are required to study ancient civilizations, develop themes related to their questions and concerns and ask them how they can integrate a study of ancient Egypt into those themes. For example, themes of prejudice or power can govern an investigation into the class structure of ancient Egypt. A technology theme can guide the analysis of pyramid construction and mummification techniques. Disease and medical conditions in Egypt can be explored under the theme of wellness.

As you use the curriculum integration model, you will find that students frequently learn the content they are supposed to learn, in an environment in which they have ownership of that content. They are, in turn, linking the content to issues that are relevant to their lives. For example, they see that power issues in ancient Egypt are not much different from those encountered in their own lives and world today.

Can you use this model in your own classroom while still being true to curriculum mandates? Absolutely. Read the story of one social studies teacher who did just that.

Real Learning in My Classroom? Yes!

BY J. SCOTT CLARK (1996)

Teaching: Loftiest of professions or daily drudgery? Tradition of Socrates or foolish frustration? Most of us had hoped that we would teach students who would be thirsting for the gems of knowledge we have to offer them; yet, how often has it felt more like we are casting pearls before swine? In vain we have sought a new teaching method, a new gimmick, a different school, improved technology, a better group of students, the perfect textbook, some way to motivate our pupils into becoming real students, perhaps even scholars. But is our quest all in vain? A recent, ongoing experience has led me to believe that that goal is attainable, right in my own, everyday middle school classroom. My hope is that the following account will provide enough details so that anyone can replicate my success and experience my joy.

In September 1996, I entered my twenty-eighth year as a middle school social studies teacher. I cared deeply about my students and worked well with my interdisciplinary team, but I was prepared for another year of wondering how much my students would really learn, how much they would become engaged in what I had to offer them. I even signed up for one more of those "educational" courses. (You know, the kind where you listen to the drivel from another "expert" professor who you think could never survive an hour with thirty energetic adolescents.)

Little did I realize the "door" she would open for me. Her message was simple and concise: "It's the curriculum, stupid!" She even plastered it across the front of the room with a banner and flaunted it on her baseball cap. She thought the curriculum was the problem? Was she crazy?

Perhaps, but Professor Trudy Knowles introduced me to a small and growing group of reformers led by James Beane who have come to realize that student apathy and uninvolvement cannot be remedied by how we teach, what books we use, or the introduction of new technology in the classroom. No, the solution to our problem lies in the simple but radical notion of curriculum change. They do not simply mean selecting another choice from the menu or even teaching it in conjunction with one's teammates. Instead they suggest that the menu be more relevant to the real world, to the concerns of both adults and adolescents. They suggest that the menu choices be partially determined by student input (What, democracy in the classroom?). They suggest that the classroom experience will be embraced by students when it offers them an opportunity to grapple with the serious, real, and overwhelming issues of our day. Since these issues are not arbitrarily broken down into academic disciplines, neither can educators dissect them into math, social studies, science, and language arts. Teachers must help students to pursue these concerns utilizing all of the disciplines simultaneously. Above all, they must allow their students to seek, inquire, question, probe, and discover what even the teachers may not know. Then and only then will we witness the student involvement and learning of our dreams.

Aha! Pie in the sky, I thought. I would need the cooperation and support of my teaching team, department head, principal, students, and their parents. What materials could I use? How could grades be determined in this process where inquiry would be its own end instead of tests and quizzes? Were my students "good" enough for this? Could I ever implement Beane's ideas in the less-than-ideal conditions in which real teachers labor? My optimism and frustration led me to try.

My "recipe" for success? It is really quite simple. Permission to experiment was readily granted, especially since any success could be shared by supervisors, no new technology was required, and the purchase of a new textbook could be delayed even longer. When I approached my students with the notion that we would, together, actually seek answers to the important issues of their world, enthusiasm was overwhelming. In fact, the decision was made not to stop at answers but to actually attempt to implement solutions. They desperately wanted to make a difference, to improve the world they live in.

What topics would we pursue? Students, individually and privately, listed all of the pressing problems they could think of. Taking only one "area" at a time, they listed all the problems of world, country, region, school, family, and self. Problems already listed under a previous area were not repeated as they moved down this list of progressively narrower areas. Already they felt that an adult was truly interested in them and their opinions. These private lists were huge, even the lists of students who usually refused to participate in anything I asked them to do. We then consolidated their individual lists into a gigantic whole-class list. We covered one area at a time and filled up all of our blackboard space. At this point, I was little more than a recording secretary who helped students clarify ideas and refine terminology. No attempt was made to edit or criticize ideas. Everyone felt validated when her/his problems were accepted. The students were happy when they found that others shared their concerns and fears, and proud when they pointed out problems that others had not thought of. So far, everyone was a winner.

The next step was critical to our success or failure, to the acceptance of our program by all those "outsiders" like principals and parents. Which one of these problems (well over a hundred in each class group) would they select to study? If their choices proved frivolous, no one would take them seriously. If I exercised control and led them toward the problems I wanted them to study, the students would not take me seriously. Was I in over my head? No!

At the end of three days, each class narrowed its list to the seven or eight most serious problems. They did it while I acted only as facilitator. We had to design ways to reach consensus rather than alienating class members. Simple voting that could result in winners and losers was not acceptable.

We began by my reading aloud, slowly and carefully, the entire class list while each student quietly wrote down the problems that were his or her personal top ten to fifteen. I wrote all of these on the board, immediately narrowing our whole-class lists to approximately twenty-five. Students removed problems that seemed less pressing and elevated ones that were more crucial by annotating their personal top ten, marking the three that they considered of paramount importance and crossing out the three that they were most willing to concede. Students suggested such strategies as combining and enlarging to further narrow the lists. After much discussion about the major issues of today (discussions that floored me with their depth, complexity, and passion and for which my presence was totally irrelevant) students reached agreement on their final lists.

What adult leaders would have chosen better? Their class lists were composed of such problems as crime and violence, war, prejudice, disease, rights and freedom, environment, immigration, starvation, employment, poverty and welfare, taxes, drugs, and education. Not a single frivolous problem had even made it to their semifinal lists. Students really are involved with and tuned into their world. All I needed was to have faith in them.

What next? We had to begin our actual inquiry, our problem solving. The only obstacle was that no one had ever entrusted such a task to these eighth graders before. How should they go about it? Here was a job made to order for the teacher in me. After a brief bit of research and some collaboration with my colleagues, I designed a chart that outlined a step-by-step method for solving any problem. It includes:

- careful elaboration of the problem itself
- discovery of the causes
- proposal and analysis of the solutions
- decision as to which solutions to use
- formulation of a plan of action
- implementation of the plan
- a reporting procedure as to what and how it was accomplished.

A simple, hypothetical problem (stolen family car) provided the basis for a practice exercise in using the problem-solving chart. This practice exercise gave both the students and myself a chance to try out our new roles within a classroom. I had to stop thinking of myself as the person with the answers and they had to begin thinking and taking responsibility for their own results. Small cooperative learning groups, often preceded by initial attempts by each individual student, seemed an ideal way to structure the class. It also provided me with more information about how each student performed in a group so that I could form more effective groups for our real projects that would follow.

The choice of our first inquiry topic was determined by the immediate availability of materials. Since prejudice was on each class list and there were ample materials at hand, the selection was easy. My role included material collection and selection, a role I shared more and more with the students as they became accustomed to our new curriculum approach. Textbooks, short stories, newspaper and magazine articles, library materials, computer-generated information, and community resources were all possible materials for students to use as they pursued solutions. I discovered that it was of paramount importance for me to act as a facilitator so that the students could pursue their own inquiries and solutions. I asked only open-ended questions that no one even expected me to answer, for they were coming to realize that only their answers matter.

But what about grades? Oh yes, administrators feel the need for them, parents insist on them, and even students want feedback about how they are doing. This new curriculum holds the promise that all students will do well. We still need, however, to document that progress.

Since tests obviously would not do that, I utilized four methods: informal teacher observations; daily journal entries in which students recorded their accomplishments, reflections, and feelings; notebooks that students utilized to record their problem-solving process; and the actual solutions that students devised, contained in written reports documenting what they accomplished (a type of portfolio). This system may not be as mathematically precise as we are used to, but it offers a deeper and more realistic reflection of what a student has really achieved. It even had beneficial side effects. Classes ended on a reflective note as every student spent the last five minutes quietly writing in his or her journal to sum up what had been learned that day. As the time of departure approached, I was surrounded by a sea of hands beckoning me to stamp their daily entries with a "smiley face," my way of acknowledging and thanking them for their participation.

What has all of this accomplished? I am no longer in the memorization business. I am not the game show host who has the answers written out on little cards. I do not have to struggle to motivate bored students. This is real life simply transplanted into a classroom. Real people are seeking real answers to real concerns. As long as it remains their search, the students are the source of their own motivation.

My students are actively engaged in class; they are exploring complex subjects utilizing primary source materials; and they have finally entered into the realms of intellectual problem solving. They feel vibrant and alive because they are not just studying for grades but are actually changing their world. They feel empowered because their opinions and judgments are being actively solicited on a daily basis. They are beginning to understand that problems of this magnitude require cooperation if we are ever going to solve them. Their journal entries and parents' comments reflect the involvement and interest that has been stimulated. They are preparing themselves for the challenge of the twenty-first century, and I am privileged to witness their progress.

Concluding Reflections

As we look at the realities of young adolescence, we are convinced that a curriculum integration model most clearly meets the needs of the middle level learner. It directly responds to their concerns about the world as they struggle to find meaning. It addresses cognitive, emotional, social, and physical developmental issues. It responds to issues of ethnic diversity, multiple intelligences, and differing abilities. It focuses on high-level conceptual thinking in addition to the development of necessary skills. And it infuses the classroom with democratic ideals. Who can argue with this?

Many middle level educators may agree with our conclusion but see the problems in its implementation mentioned above—discounting of professional training, presence of a mandated curriculum, tyranny of textbooks, anxious parents, and legislative pressures. Some educators believe that the obstacles are so great that curriculum reform will never be implemented on a wide scale and that the middle school movement would be better served by a focus on instruction rather than curriculum. Realizing that changing what we teach is a hard sell, Gatewood (1998) advocates focusing on the way we teach.

> While curriculum integration is an important consideration for middle level educators, it should not currently be our number one priority. The issue of classroom instruction is much more critical. Most middle school instruction is still primarily didactic. It is characterized by lecture, teacher-led discussion, student worksheets and other forms of seat work, and whole group activities with little differentiation for individual student differences. . . . More emphasis should be placed on experiential, hands-on learning and on higher order thinking through active dialogue and discussion, open-ended questioning, and use of primary data sources in testing of hypotheses and reflective thinking. (41)

What we teach is connected to how we teach, which is ultimately linked to what is actually learned. As you read the next chapter, instead of thinking about the traditional roles of teachers in middle school classrooms, try to focus on issues of real learning in a context of collaboration.

References

BEANE, J. A. 1993. *A Middle School Curriculum: From Rhetoric to Reality.* Columbus, OH: National Middle School Association.

———. 1997. *Curriculum Integration: Designing the Core of Democratic Education.* New York: Teachers College Press.

———. 1998. "A Process for Collaborative Teacher-Student Planning." *The Core Teacher* 48, no. 3: 3–4.

BORDEAUX, R. 1992–1993. Unpublished poetry for class project. Sinte Gleska University, Mission, SD.

CLARK, S. 1996. "Real Learning in My Classroom? Yes!" Unpublished Manuscript. Westfield State College, Westfield, MA.

———. 1997. Unpublished Presentation Materials. Westfield State College, Westfield, MA.

DAVID, R., ed. 1998. *Moving Forward from the Past: Early Writings and Current Reflections of Middle School Founders.* Columbus, OH: National Middle School Association.

DICKINSON, T., ed. 1993. *Readings in Middle School Curriculum: A Continuing Conversation.* Columbus, OH: National Middle School Association.

EICHHORN, D. H. 1967. "New Knowledge of 10- Through 13-Year Olds." In *Moving Forward From the Past: Early Writings and Current Reflections of Middle School Founders,* ed. R. David. 1998. Columbus OH: National Middle School Association. 43–53.

FORBES, E. 1944. *Johnny Tremain.* Boston: Houghton Mifflin.

FRANK, A. 1967. *The Diary of a Young Girl.* New York: Doubleday.

GATEWOOD, T. 1998. "How Valid Is Integrated Curriculum in Today's Middle Schools?" *Middle School Journal* 29, no. 4, 38–41.

NATIONAL MIDDLE SCHOOL ASSOCIATION. 1995. *This We Believe: Developmentally Responsive Middle Level Schools.* Columbus OH: National Middle School Association.

POWELL, R. R. 1999. "Reflections on Integrative Curriculum: A Conversation with Camille Barr and Molly Maloy." *Middle School Journal* 31, no. 2: 25–34.

RASKIN, E. 1978. *The Westing Game.* New York: Puffin Books.

SWAIM, S. 1993. "Curriculum Change—The Time is Now." In *Readings in Middle School Curriculum: A Continuing Conversation*, ed. T. Dickinson. Columbus, OH: National Middle School Association, xi–xiii.

TOEPFER, C. 1969. "Curricular Imperatives for the Middle School." In *Moving Forward From the Past: Early Writings and Current Reflections of Middle School Founders*, ed. R. David. 1998. Columbus OH: National Middle School Association, 134–139.

SIX

Facilitating Meaningful Learning

You are always going to come up with your own way of learning something.

JESS, EIGHTH GRADE

When one approach doesn't work, you don't give up! You've got to go back into that bag and keep pulling out different approaches until the children learn.

MARIA, FIFTH-GRADE TEACHER

The curriculum integration model advocated in Chapter 5 may have challenged your views of curriculum development. This model also runs contrary to traditional views of how students learn. The curriculum integration approach places less emphasis on your role as a content area specialist and more emphasis on helping students make connections among relevant topics. During the school day, students will not move from subject area to subject area but from  learning experience to another. But whether you design curriculum and activities collaboratively with students, develop instruction as part of a team, or teach a separate content area, the lessons you plan and the activities you choose determine whether meaningful learning will occur.

In *This We Believe* (1995), NMSA advocates instruction that employs "varied teaching and learning approaches" (24). According to this document, "The distinctive developmental and learning characteristics of young adolescents provide the foundation for selecting teaching strategies, just as they do for designing curriculum. Teaching techniques should enhance and accommodate the diverse skills, abilities, and knowledge of young adolescents, cultivate multiple intelligences, and capitalize on students' individual learning styles" (24). Instructional practices in middle schools should focus on what we know about the learning needs of young adolescents coupled with what we know about how learning occurs.

Time for Reflection
- What is learning?
- How does learning occur?
- How is learning out of school different from learning in school?
- What specific characteristics of young adolescents might affect their ability to learn? How?

How Learning Occurs

Recent scientific discoveries on cognition and how the brain works impact our understanding about how learning occurs and the teachers' role in the learning process (Caine and Caine 1994; Jensen 1998). In addition, developing an understanding of how we construct knowledge and the role that socialization plays in that construction help teachers make better curricular and instructional decisions in the context of young adolescent development.

Brain-Based Learning

Caine and Caine (1994) describe some of the elements of learning that coincide with how the brain operates. Notice the connections between these principles, young adolescent developmental needs, and the curriculum integration model.

1. "Learning Engages the Entire Physiology" (88). Learning is not just a cognitive process. Teachers should consider physical, emotional, and social factors as well. Although relevant for all ages, this principle is particularly significant for young adolescents because of their growth in all areas.

2. "The Search for Meaning is Innate" (89). All people attempt to make meaning of the circumstances of their lives. Curricular and instructional decisions should establish the necessary conditions for students to create meaning.

3. "The Search for Meaning Occurs Through Patterning" (89). In order to find meaning, students must begin to see the relationship between what they are studying and what is happening in their lives. Finding these relationships requires strategies that engage students in using problem solving and critical thinking processes.

4. "Emotions are Critical to Patterning" (90). Emotions may have as much or more to do with what students learn as their cognitive abilities do, particularly in young adolescents who experience a multitude of emotions each day. Teachers must create emotionally supportive environments in order to assure that students engage in meaningful learning.

5. "The Brain Processes Parts and Wholes Simultaneously" (91). Bolstered by the books edited by E. D. Hirsch, Jr. (1993), *What Your First Grader Needs to Know*, up through *What Your Sixth Grader Needs To Know*, some teachers believe learning involves mastering isolated skills and memorizing information. Memorizing isolated bits of information disconnected from general principles and broad concepts limits students' cognitive potential and their opportunities for true understanding.

Effective teachers help students learn skills and knowledge within the context of genuine learning situations.

6. "Learning Always Involves Conscious and Unconscious Processes" (92). Teachers must provide time for students to reflect on newfound discoveries in a way that encourages them to accept new theories as they alter previous beliefs. With the emergence of formal and abstract thinking, young adolescents begin to reflect on their own learning.

7. "Learning is Enhanced by Challenge and Inhibited by Threat" (94). Caine and Caine suggest that teachers create a learning environment for students in which they are in a state of "relaxed alertness" (70). In such a classroom, students are emotionally, cognitively, and socially safe. It is a place where students know they are cared for and valued. In such an environment, students are comfortable engaging in challenging learning opportunities. In Chapter 4 we discussed ways to create this safe haven for learning through getting to know your students and developing trust in the classroom.

Constructivism: A Theory About Learning

We constantly construct knowledge and meaning throughout our lives as we are confronted with problems, new ideas, and new knowledge. A toddler learning how to stack blocks, a first grader learning the connection between letters and words, a fourth grader exploring maps, or a seventh grader examining the meaning of prejudice are all constructing knowledge about their world. It is evident from looking at the principles of brain-based learning that in order to construct meaning, students must have opportunities to manipulate ideas and materials. Teachers can't make students construct knowledge—they do this naturally and without external prodding. Teachers can, however, set up an environment that promotes active learning through providing authentic hands-on and minds-on learning experiences within a social context. Michael, a seventh grader, told us, "You've got to learn by doing it. You can't learn about it by taking notes." An eighth grade student concurred: "I think kids would learn a lot better if you do something hands-on."

Several significant differences exist between learning in a traditional classroom and learning in a classroom that models the constructivist philosophy. A traditional classroom is characterized by a focus on discrete, often unrelated, skills. Teachers are viewed as dispensers of information and follow fixed curricula, guided by textbooks and curriculum guides. The emphasis in a constructivist classroom is on general principles and concepts. Teachers support learning by providing materials and ideas for students to manipulate and facilitating personal and group reflections as students interact with the material. Teachers carefully introduce and embed needed skills as students engage in the process of exploration. Brooks and Brooks (1993) summarize the principle of constructivism this way, "We look not for what students can repeat, but for what they can generate, demonstrate, and exhibit" (16).

In designing instruction so that students have opportunities to construct their own knowledge, the important consideration is that students are not told what they should find, but are given the opportunity to make sense out of the information themselves. For example, students experiment with pendulums to determine what factor affects its rate of speed. Students analyze lists of words to determine spelling patterns. Students explore music to develop an understanding of a cultural era. Students look for patterns in the survey data they collect. Teachers do not sit on the sidelines as students manipulate and explore ideas and materials. In addition to setting up the conditions for student exploration, they point students in the right direction, providing frequent feedback to assure accurate understanding of principles.

Constructivist classrooms are practical instructional designs that take into account brain-based learning theory as well as what we know about the developing adolescent. When students are provided with opportunities to build their own understandings through interacting with the environment, their knowledge about topics is enhanced in a meaningful way.

Socialization and the Learning Process

Brain-based learning, constructivist theory, and the needs of the young adolescent all point to the positive role that socialization can play in the learning process. Young adolescents will talk to each other in the halls, during class, during breaks, at lunch, and on the telephone in the evenings. It should not be difficult then for teachers to get students talking in the classroom about learning. We have made a good start when we collaborate with students about curricular issues. This collaboration must continue in our instruction.

School is the place where students can learn to work collaboratively with others in developing questions, reaching consensus, solving problems, creating projects, and resolving disagreements. School is where we learn to become team players and to understand that there are differences in the way people think. As Wolfe and Brandt (1998) suggest, "learning is enhanced when the environment provides [students] with the opportunity to discuss their thinking out loud, to bounce their ideas off of their peers, and to produce collaborative work" (11).

Never assume that students already know how to work collaboratively. Many students may have had cooperative learning experiences in elementary school, but often these past experiences resulted in failure and frustration. To ensure success at the middle level, ample time in the first nine weeks of the school year should be devoted to helping students develop interpersonal strategies needed to progress successfully as a team. Pairing students together for short time periods to work on small projects is a beginning strategy for encouraging students to trust each other and develop productive working relationships. Following this exercise, teachers should facilitate a discussion on the pitfalls and advantages students face when working with others. Sharing concerns about the process of teamwork early in the year may help students to more successfully navigate future team efforts. Student teams may become the primary learning group in a classroom.

The writing workshop (Atwell 1998) offers the opportunity for students to construct their own knowledge about writing while collaborating with others. Writing workshops feature opportunities for students to choose writing topics, student-to-student conferencing, peer revision and editing sessions, and one-to-one conferences with the teacher.

Literature circles represent another example of a collaborative activity (Daniels 1994). In a literature circle, four to six students engage in critical analyses of books that they choose based on their interests. Literature circles present opportunities for students to process information, create meaning from text, and use critical thinking skills.

Research-team investigations and group oral presentations are other examples of collaborative activities that lead to meaningful learning. Groups of students first analyze primary source materials to generate ideas about an event, culture, or historical period. Information is interpreted from diverse and multiple points of view. Students then collaborate on the best way to present their understandings to the rest of the class.

The real value of social learning occurs when students share their questions about issues, offer alternative points of view, devise creative solutions to problems, and provide feedback to each other on the products of their learning. Young adolescents are also more likely to take the risks associated with learning new concepts and principles when they have opportunities to collaborate.

It is not surprising that when structured correctly, collaborative learning provides many benefits. Slavin (1991) has described some of the advantages of collaborative learning:

- enhanced achievement
- improved self-esteem
- improved relationships among students of different races, genders, and abilities
- greater acceptance of students with special needs

Effective educators take advantage of the socialization needs of young adolescents by designing collaborative student learning experiences.

The Teacher's Role

> To make teaching and learning work . . . . teachers must develop an alternative approach to instructional planning beyond "covering the text" or "creating activities that students will like."
>
> TOMLINSON (1999, 14)

> The role of the teacher is to ask questions—constantly! Teachers offer timely intervention when students need help, directing students to resources, suggesting other sources of help in the classroom and out.
>
> MIKE MUIR (QUOTED IN BRAZEE AND CAPELLUTI 1994, 70)

> The teacher is literally a designer who takes bigger ideas and fashions them into learning experiences so young adolescents can learn.
>
> MARY BILODEAU-CALLAN (QUOTED IN BRAZEE AND CAPELLUTI 1994, 71)

An understanding of the learning process can help teachers make better decisions about what goes on in the classroom. And yet, often, after repeated hours of teacher planning, numerous homework assignments, and all that grading, we dare to ask, "Do you suppose students are really learning?"

Learning is ultimately an individual endeavor. Each student encounters new ideas and information and constructs meaning based on his or her own understanding of the world. The teacher, however, is not passive in this endeavor. Teachers play a vital role in helping students acquire essential skills and concepts they need. Although they may collaborate with students regarding instructional strategies, it is ultimately the teacher who must plan and design the school day.

Effective instructional practice, however, involves more than designing lesson plans to fit the curriculum guides, implementing teaching strategies, and following the steps of the Madeline Hunter (1984) model of instruction in lesson presentation. Teachers who limit themselves to these traditional activities are ignoring the latest research on cognition and discounting the ability of young adolescents to search for their own understanding.

In talking to students it becomes apparent that they also want something other than traditional forms of teaching. A seventh-grade student told us: "Spend more time and try to do creative things, like hands-on. Have kids have their own opinion on something, not just say, 'This is the way it is.' There are always two ways to learn something. Maybe one way is always easier but you are always going to come up with your own way of learning something so I think they should give kids more of an opinion. They shouldn't just be so out of the book."

Teachers who engage in effective instructional practices use everything they know about their content area, learning, young adolescent development, their students, and instruction in order to make the best choices every day.

Establishing Essential Outcomes

One teacher responsibility is to clarify skills and strategies that students need to learn. Although students will have considerable input with respect to classroom learning, Voltz (1999) explains that one "important role of the teachers is to conduct knowledge and skill analyses to determine what, if any, important information or aspects of the curriculum have been omitted in student generated topics and activities" (33). The list of desired outcomes does not need to be extensive; however, it should represent a set of cognitive processes that will assure student growth beyond middle school. Below is an example. Students will develop the ability to:

- communicate their questions and concerns
- hypothesize responses to some of their questions
- develop observation skills and make inferences about these observations
- analyze topics from different points of view
- apply research techniques to gather and analyze primary and secondary sources
- apply problem-solving strategies using both creative and critical thinking.

As you collaborate with students on topics and strategies, an understanding of essential outcomes will help you and your students more effectively structure learning activities.

Facilitators in Action

Teachers take on a variety of roles throughout the school day. The primary role is that of a guide who facilitates the students' search for meaning. "Teacher as facilitator" is perhaps an overused metaphor that some have even interpreted as a teacher cop-out on instructional responsibilities. Being a facilitator, however, requires a great deal of effort, energy, and perseverance. Indeed, in the facilitator role teachers take on more demands than they would in a more traditional instructional model. Under the curriculum integration model, the role is especially challenging. As Nesin and Lounsbury (1999) explain: "[Teachers] have to assist in designing experiments, refining surveys, locating resources, inventing games, resolving conflicts, analyzing data, and delegating responsibility. In addition, they deliver appropriate lectures, organize parts of the unit, monitor student involvement, and assess learning on a daily basis. Teachers also have to create strategies for activities and learning they cannot possibly anticipate" (34).

As a facilitator, some of your primary responsibilities will be to help students develop themes, create the questions they hope to answer through the study of the themes, and generate activities through which they can explore their questions. You will then develop a daily plan that will support students as they conduct their inquiry. Your own academic strengths and pedagogical awareness will come into play as you provide historical background knowledge or sources of information and embed learning skills and intended outcomes into the study of the topic.

Some teachers use the "KWL" approach in helping students get a handle on their topic. They begin by asking students what they already *know* about a topic and then generate ideas about what they *want* to know. As the facilitator, you will assist students in narrowing their ideas into ones that can be reasonably researched and help them generate ways to locate information from primary and secondary sources. The final step in the KWL process is for students to identify what they have *learned* and to present that information in a meaningful way.

You have several instructional responsibilities during students' search for information. You will teach them the necessary skills to complete their research. Together with students, you may determine that more background information is needed on a topic. You will collaborate on what knowledge is needed and how students can best acquire that knowledge. At times, that may mean direct instruction on a specific topic.

When you collaborate with students on activities, they may suggest a wide variety of ways to approach the acquisition of knowledge. Many students want to do some kind of project to obtain and demonstrate knowledge. As Brodhagen (1998) explains, "Projects . . . provide students opportunities to use multiple resources including technology, popular culture, common 'experts' (people in their personal community who know much about a topic), multicultural resources, and personal experiences" (51).

For example, students might want to interview experts. You could conduct a minilesson on how to generate questions or conduct an interview and then help them set up the interviews. Students might want to conduct a school survey. You will help them develop survey questions and analyze, interpret, and report data.

Two outcomes that you may have identified are improved ability to read and analyze texts and advanced development of writing skills. You might help students choose appropriate novels that address the theme being studied and demonstrate how a literature circle (Daniels 1994) works. Students might decide to create a newsletter for the school to present the information they have learned. In order to improve students' writing skills, you might provide skill sessions on such topics as appropriate citations, accurate paraphrasing, use of correct writing conventions, or peer revising skills (Atwell 1998).

This type of instruction requires attention to each student's needs and flexibility in teacher response. It is necessary for teachers to engage in frequent conferences with individuals or groups to set goals, establish timelines, and monitor progress toward a final product. Students can focus on their learning during these conferences by responding to teacher questions such as:

- What do you hope to learn as a result of studying this topic?
- What are some ways in which you could demonstrate your learning?
- How does what you know compare with what you would like to know?
- Who would you like to share your new knowledge with once you have researched the topic?
- How would you evaluate your final product?

Students are encouraged during conferences to explain their work, talk about their explorations, and seek new avenues of research. Your collaboration and conferencing with students becomes paramount in deciding how they will demonstrate their newfound knowledge to others. Students may need extensive instruction, guidance, and feedback as they develop final presentations, pieces of writing, works of art, or scientific demonstrations. Conferences that include parents encourage students to take ownership of their own learning.

As you can see, teachers are highly involved in structuring learning processes. Although you want students to have substantial input, what happens during the school day is ultimately up to you. Your repertoire of strategies must be immense. Brodhagen (1998) discusses some of the instructional strategies that teachers use: "Cooperative learning groups can be a powerful instructional strategy when used correctly. Direct teaching can be effective when used appropriately. Presenting information through both visual and auditory methods increases retention of material. The use of advanced organizers, anticipatory sets, or scaffolding helps students understand and remember more when ideas or information are connected to prior learning" (50–51). Nesin and Lounsbury (1999) observed that although many of these strategies can be viewed as traditional and may be used in any classroom, in curriculum integration classrooms "strategies and activities selected result from student-teacher planning rather than teachers' unilateral decisions" (34).

Effective teaching requires extensive pedagogical knowledge. You will need to continue to develop background knowledge in your area of expertise while becoming more immersed in other content areas. In addition, you must continue to grow in your ability to accept and adjust to how each student learns and how to encourage further social, emotional, and cognitive growth.

Recognizing Diversity

A good teacher is one who understands your needs—understands what you need as a student. I'm not saying they have to sit down and write, 'Jason needs this, Tom needs this, Anne needs this, Marie needs this.' But, they have to be able to know if I don't understand something.

JASON, SIXTH GRADER

It is easy to recognize the physical differences of young adolescents as they enter a classroom; however, perceiving cognitive, social, and emotional differences is challenging, and it is difficult to respond to these differences on a daily basis. Students are as different in the way they learn as they are in the way they look. They differ in the way they process and understand knowledge and in the way they construct meaning from knowledge. Sally, an eighth-grade teacher, revealed the diversity she sees in her students: "Each child learns differently. One child might have only a two-minute attention span. Another child might come to school with a host of issues and just be completely exhausted." Students see this diversity also. Jake, a sixth grader, told us, "There is such a wide range of smartness in the school in each class. It's hard because some kids move faster than others, and they [the teachers] have to know the needs of some kids."

Traditional curriculum design and many traditional teaching strategies do not account for the diversity of students' learning needs. The belief that "one size fits all" when it comes to preparing students for life after school results in every student being exposed to the same curricula, reading the same book, receiving the same assignments, acquiring information through the same instructional model, and completing the same tests to demonstrate growth. This philosophy and accompanying

119

instructional practices are accepted by many as the most successful method of educating students. But using the same methods for all students will only ensure that some are not successful. Standardized methods create frustration for many students and their teachers.

Jensen (1998) describes one instance of this frustration: "Julie's teacher spends a lot of time reteaching because she doesn't teach in ways that match how Julie's brain learns. This mismatch creates frustration, under performance, and hopelessness" (41). Both the teacher and student are frustrated by the inability to have their needs met— the teacher, who wants to help Julie succeed but is afraid to let go of traditional views of learning, and Julie, who wants to experience academic success.

Recognizing diversity in learning means that teachers understand that each student has a unique way of accessing, processing, and applying information. Learning preferences and differences may be based on environmental conditions, on genetic, neurological, or other physical challenges, or on a combination of environmental and physical factors. A student's learning preferences may differ from another's based on broad issues such as developmental level, gender, race, ethnicity, socioeconomic class, or native language. Learning differences may be very specific, such as a preference for learning from parts to whole or vice versa, the need for social interaction versus independent study, the preference for analytical methods of learning, the need to write to enhance learning, or the need to engage in physical movement when learning. Variations in personal interests, learning disabilities, and differences in degrees of background knowledge also impact learning preferences (Tomlinson 1999).

Put simply, every teacher must accept and respond in a way that recognizes that every student is simultaneously at-risk and gifted. The causes of individual differences are not as important as the responsibility for teachers to assure that every student has opportunities to succeed at learning—daily.

Wilhelm (1997) describes what he does as a language arts teacher: "I study every student who comes into my classroom. To do less would be to not take each student with the seriousness she or he deserves" (28). As you become acquainted with your students, you will begin to perceive their learning preferences. You will see how students process information, you will notice the kinds of activities they need in order to be challenged, and wisely, you will assist students in designing learning experiences that capitalize on their strengths and build on their weaknesses. You will take your instructional cues from your students, being sensitive to their needs and challenges.

If teachers take the time to help students become reflective, young adolescents will become sensitive to their own learning preferences. Providing examples of different ways to approach a task and opportunities for student choice promotes the development of self-awareness. As students better understand their own learning preferences and differences, they learn to construct knowledge in more meaningful ways. They engage in projects and activities that promote their way of learning and allow them to be more successful at school.

Teachers' attitudes, philosophies, and ultimately actions in recognizing differences in students determine the degree of success that students will experience. Tomlinson (1999) outlines three central beliefs of teachers who promote what she describes as "differentiated learning." Teachers

1. expect all students to grow, and support their continual growth
2. offer all students the opportunity to explore central understandings and skills at degrees of difficulty that escalate consistently as they develop their understanding and skill
3. offer all students tasks that look—and are—equally interesting, equally important, and equally engaging. (12)

No standardized model for designing learning experiences can meet the needs of all students in every classroom. Understanding, validating, and responding to student learning differences is an imperative responsibility of professional educators. All students have a right to succeed, and teachers must provide the necessary environment for that to happen. Traditional whole-class instruction makes the creation of such an environment unlikely. When you plan curriculum and instruction collaboratively with students, you are better able to meet their individual needs.

Living with Mandates

Many of you will be employed in schools that mandate specific skills and topics to be covered in a certain grade. You might even be told what novels students must read. In addition, you may be genuinely concerned and worried about making sure students know the content that will be on the required state achievement tests. These realities and concerns may make you reluctant to use a curriculum model and instructional strategies that are developed through substantial student input. Many teachers, however, have discovered that collaborative planning with students has, in fact, raised achievement levels. Alexander, Carr, and McAvoy (1995) described what they discovered when they engaged their sixth grade students in designing their own curriculum and instructional strategies. "In most areas we found that these sixth graders met or exceeded the content coverage of previous classes. Some of what they learned arose from student inquiries and some from teacher givens. The big bonus was all the other learning that took place simultaneously" (56). The other learning that took place included high levels of thinking, cooperative skills, and independence and responsibility for learning. And according to the teachers, "These lessons were not learned at the expense of 'traditional content'" (56).

We are fully aware of the position in which teachers are sometimes placed when they don't cover the curriculum or complete the textbook; however, time, textbooks, and curriculum guides do not have to be impediments to implementing active learning activities within your own classroom. If you are in a school with departmentalized subject areas, as many of you are or will be, you still have the primary responsibility of meeting students' learning needs within the context of your subject area. Despite the mandates of your subject area, you may still engage students in making curricular decisions and encourage them to select among several methods of learning and assessment. After you collaborate with students to develop themes based on their questions and concerns, you can then show them the list of mandated topics and have them work with you on developing ways to integrate those topics into their investigations. A traditional school structure is no excuse for refusing to use effective research-based pedagogical principles.

Concluding Reflections

Being a teacher is a complex task. You will not find a recipe that tells you what ingredients to use in order to be successful. We must first remember the young adolescent population with whom we are working. Young adolescents are vibrant and alive, curious and questioning, passionate and intense. If we can model their vibrancy, curiosity, and passion and see learning through their eyes, we have taken the first step toward facilitating meaningful learning. Couple that with our extensive content and pedagogical knowledge as well as the flexibility to use what we know in response to student needs, and we will be able to develop an environment where students will truly be encouraged to construct knowledge to make sense of their world.

The manner in which students learn, the content they learn, and the way that teachers determine the extent to which students create meaning are closely connected. The next chapter will assist you in developing an understanding of strategies for assessing student progress that support the creation of meaningful classroom learning environments.

References

ALEXANDER, W., D. CARR, AND K. MCAVOY. 1995. *Student-Oriented Curriculum: Asking the Right Questions.* Columbus, OH: National Middle School Association.

ATWELL, N. 1998. *In the Middle: New Understandings About Writing, Reading, and Learning.* 2nd ed. Portsmouth, NH: Heinemann.

BRAZEE, E., AND J. CAPELLUTI. 1994. *Second Generation Curriculum: What and How We Teach at the Middle Level.* Topsfield, MA: New England League of Middle Schools.

BRODHAGEN, B. 1998. "Varied Teaching and Learning Approaches." *Middle School Journal* 29, no. 3: 49–52.

BROOKS, J. G., AND M. G. BROOKS. 1993. *In Search of Understanding: The Case for Constructivist Classrooms.* Alexandria, VA: Association for Supervision and Curriculum Development.

CAINE, R. N., AND G. CAINE. 1994. *Making Connections: Teaching and the Human Brain*. Menlo Park, CA: Addison Wesley.

DANIELS, H. 1994. *Literature Circles: Voice and Choice in the Student-Centered Classroom*. York, ME: Stenhouse Publishers.

HIRSCH, E. D., JR., ED. 1993. *What Your First Grader Needs to Know*. New York: Delta.

———. 1993. *What Your Sixth Grader Needs to Know*. New York: Delta.

HUNTER, M. 1984. "Knowing, Teaching, and Supervising." In *Using What We Know About Teaching*, ed. P. Horsford. Alexandria, VA: Association for Supervision and Curriculum Development.

JENSEN, E. 1998. "How Julie's Brain Learns." *Educational Leadership* 56, no. 3: 41–45.

NESIN, G. AND J. LOUNSBURY. 1999. *Curriculum Integration: Twenty Questions—With Answers*." Atlanta, GA: Georgia Middle School Association.

NATIONAL MIDDLE SCHOOL ASSOCIATION. 1995. *This We Believe: Developmentally Responsive Middle Level Schools*. Columbus, OH: National Middle School Association.

SLAVIN, R. E. 1991. "Synthesis of Research on Cooperative Learning." *Educational Leadership* 48, no. 5: 71–77, 79–82.

TOMLINSON, C. A. 1999. "Mapping a Route Toward Differentiated Instruction." *Educational Leadership* 57, no. 1: 12–16.

VOLTZ, D. L. 1999. "Empowering Diverse Learners at the Middle Level." *Middle School Journal* 30, no. 4: 29–36.

WILHELM, J. D. 1997. *"You Gotta BE the Book": Teaching Engaged and Reflective Reading with Adolescents*. New York: Teachers College Press.

WOLFE, P., AND R. BRANDT. 1998. "What Do We Know from Brain Research?" *Education Leadership* 56, no. 3: 8–13.

SEVEN

Assessment that Promotes Active Learning

I went to school where we didn't have grades, and we didn't have tests. We never got a report card. I was much more willing to learn.

DAN, SIXTH GRADER

I think we should do projects instead of tests. They're basically the same thing, [except] projects get you more involved.

MONICA, SEVENTH GRADER

What Is Assessment?

A message posted on the campus where one of us teaches states, "Good luck on exams!" You have undoubtedly heard the same "good luck" from friends and family as you prepared to take tests. We find it humorous that *luck* would have anything to do with determining what you have learned. How can students spend so much time learning in school only to have the level of their knowledge determined by a test that relies as much on luck as it does on skill or knowledge?

The kind of assessment that takes luck to succeed involves students memorizing facts, then attempting to recall them for the test. Students who experience assessment this way usually have no knowledge of the questions they will be asked to answer until the day they take the test. This reminds us of owl pellets—you know, those small, cylinder-shaped, gray hair balls that owls regurgitate after they eat because they can't digest the hair and bones of field mice. All of us have taken a test in which we regurgitated pellets that represent the information we could not digest! We don't consider that type of assessment an accurate measure of learning. We question the validity of such tests; that is, do these traditional assessment strategies measure what they claim to measure? Do they measure what teachers want students to know?

The primary purpose of this chapter is to help you develop a more genuine view of assessment. When you think about determining what students know you may think of words such as *testing, evaluation,* or *grading.* These words do not have the same meaning as *assessment. Testing* is one way of determining what someone knows—but it is certainly not the only way, despite its frequent use. We usually think of tests as multiple-choice, true/false, or essay examinations requiring students to provide responses to a teacher's questions. Testing may come in several other formats, but the questions usually are generated from an outside source rather than from students. A weak link commonly exists between testing and what it is that teachers want students to know or be able to do as a result of studying a particular topic.

Evaluation is another word commonly used in place of assessment. Evaluation is a value assigned to student performances, and a judgment about the quality of a child's performance or product of learning (Educators in Connecticut's Pomperaug Regional School District 15 1996). Like testing, most evaluation of student learning utilizes external sources instead of being personally generated by students. The typical end products of evaluation are grades.

Grading is another word that is frequently confused with assessment. Grading is an arbitrary label teachers use to place students along a continuum from best to worst. Grades in any format such as A to F, *satisfactory,* or *at grade level* describe student performances over a period of time on a number of assessment tasks. Although grading has a strong tradition, a number of problems exist with this practice. Tombari and Borich (1999) describe some of these: "[Grades] assume equal amounts of learning have occurred for individuals who achieve the same grade, fail to acknowledge continuous progress or development in learning, and may mask an individual student's learning strengths and needs" (39). Convincing parents and other educators of the insufficiency inherent in grading is a lifetime battle. A most unfortunate fact is that grades are not motivating for many students, and grades have little to do with learning.

Assessment has a more generalized meaning than testing, grading, or evaluation. Assessment is a set of strategies for discovering what students know or can do as a result of engaging in learning experiences. It involves a number of activities designed to determine the level of student learning. Assessment is a comprehensive act that includes consideration of a student's goals for learning, processes of learning, progression toward established goals, and revision of goals when needed. All assessment should have as its primary purpose the improvement of student learning.

Time for Reflection
- Make a list of the reasons for assessing students.
- Discuss with a classmate how the reasons you've listed support young adolescents' cognitive growth.
- Describe some of the frustrations you've experienced with traditional assessment techniques.

Misuse of Assessment Strategies

Assessment *should not* be about sorting students into categories to determine their opportunities for the future; however, this is how assessment is commonly used. We do not believe that assessment should be used to motivate students. Motivation is an intrinsic thinking process initiated by students rather than an extrinsic one controlled by teachers. Meaningful assessment focuses on learning as a *process* instead of on single performances such as the taking of standardized tests. With such an emphasis on assessment, students lose interest in learning opportunities and begin to focus instead on their ability or inability to reach arbitrarily established standards. Assessment focused on specific standards emphasizes competition instead of creating diverse opportunities for student growth and academic success.

Think about your experiences with assessment: activities such as multiple-choice tests, essays, projects, or demonstrations. Do these activities contribute to students' overall knowledge or abilities? Do they demonstrate what students genuinely understand? Do assigned grades reflect what students learn or understand? What do students' scores on tests say about their actual learning? How much information do students retain after they complete a test?

As you recall your struggles and successes in mastering content information sufficiently to pass standardized, end-of-unit, and teacher-made tests, you may also remember that memorizing information for the purpose of passing a test led only to a short-term memory of most significant points. The information you memorized may have significance to you, but the way in which you learned it made it seem as if the information was useful only to the extent that knowing it helped you pass the test.

Teachers may design elaborate lessons that are engaging and meaningful, and students may gain much from the learning activities; however, when students are tested by means of a multiple-choice test, the genuine value of the content is often diminished. Students are denied opportunities to develop connections between the content they study and their lives when traditional testing formats are used. Traditional assessment instruments, due to their emphasis on simple recall, fail to encourage the development of students' abilities in the specific kinds of strategies needed to succeed in life (Schurr 1999).

Assessment should not be focused on the number of facts students have memorized but rather on meaningful learning experiences. Schurr (1999) emphasizes the importance of learning during assessment activities: "Assessment is about determining what one knows and can do and what one doesn't know and cannot do. Yet, if the true mission of teaching is to help students learn, the measurement must foster growth and development" (17).

An essential concern of ours is that assessment is *not* the end product of learning. Assessment becomes meaningful only when curriculum is designed collaboratively and students decide how they will learn information. In this scenario, assessment comprises the meaningful learning activities students engage in throughout their studies. A culminating project or demonstration integrates the essential knowledge and skills that students have obtained.

Connecting Assessment to Curriculum and Instruction

The strategies chosen for determining what students know differ considerably from those of traditional practice when *learning* is the anchor of one's assessment philosophy. Assessment practices must be closely connected to curriculum and instruction. The beliefs that a teacher holds regarding these three components affects the choice of how he or she determines what students know or are able to do as a result of learning. Separate-subject curricular design, teacher-centered instruction, and traditional testing techniques often fail to meet the criterion for connecting curriculum, instruction, and assessment in a meaningful way. These three components of learning are connected when students are actively engaged in developing the curricular focus and are involved in choosing how they will learn.

For instance, students who choose as a small group to study the source of pollution in a local stream are engaged in learning a topic of interest. Students take part in genuine learning as they develop hypotheses, determine how to collect information, analyze samples, and reach conclusions about the stream. Learning occurs through the reflective processes of determining how to design a project that demonstrates their newfound knowledge and in the method they choose to present their findings. Students' assessment decisions provide direction to purposeful learning activities. Student motivation is an end result of the powerful connection of curriculum, instruction, and assessment.

Alternative Assessment

We support *alternative assessment* activities—alternatives to the traditional standardized tests and teacher-made quizzes that characterized classrooms of the past. Alternative assessments are strategies for determining what students know or are capable of doing that don't rely on standardized, multiple-choice, short answer, true/false, or essay tests.

Students develop research skills and problem-solving abilities, think creatively, debate, engage in authentic writing experiences, and mapping activities, and collaborate successfully among themselves when they have opportunities to personalize curriculum and the ways in which they learn. As described in Chapter 6, these are the cognitive activities that students must be engaged in each day for genuine learning to occur. Traditional assessment strategies do not enable students to demonstrate the growth they have acquired as a result of engaging in these meaningful activities.

Meaningful assessment embodies the following characteristics:

- It begins with student goal setting.
- It provides choices for students in demonstrating what they know.
- It allows for flexibility in its design.
- It is developmentally appropriate for each young adolescent.
- It provides opportunities for self-evaluation.
- It encourages development of students' thinking processes.
- It creates authentic connections.
- It permits demonstrations of learning that build on strengths and weaknesses.

Students' Roles in Assessment

Goal setting is an important aspect of student curricular and assessment decision making. Young adolescents' growing abilities to assess their academic strengths and weaknesses enable them to develop a set of personal learning outcomes. Student-teacher conferencing should be conducted frequently to determine student progress in developing outcomes and to reassess goals if necessary. A copy of these outcomes should be placed in a student's portfolio as a reminder of the direction the student intends to take to reach desired ends.

Students can focus on assessment issues during student-teacher conferences by responding to these questions, suggested as part of conferences in Chapter 6:

- What do you hope to learn as a result of studying this topic?
- How might you show your understanding of this information?
- How does what you already know compare with what you'd like to know?
- Who would you like to share your new knowledge with once you have researched this topic?
- How would you evaluate your final product with respect to this topic?

Helping students develop a course of study, choose strategies for learning information, and select ways of presenting their learning to classmates, parents, and teachers is a journey that is continually evolving. Teachers must work with students to help them identify process skills and work habits they need to develop, such as analytical and research skills, time-management strategies, persistence, and collaboration with classmates (Educators in Connecticut's Pomperaug Regional School District 15 1996).

This process involves ongoing teacher guidance and conferencing, student risk-taking and experimentation, and careful design and possible redesign of final projects. Learning occurs as much in the unfolding of the process as it does in the completion of the final product or culminating performance.

Few middle level schools have adopted this type of assessment philosophy, due in part to a belief that young adolescents are not capable of independent learning. We know, however, that their emerging metacognitive abilities permit young adolescents to evaluate their performance on academic tasks. Young adolescents are able to see their mistakes and correct them without intensive teacher direction, think creatively when given opportunities for reflection, utilize analytical strategies that they had not been capable of prior to this growth period, and develop advanced questioning strategies that provide teachers with insights into their depth of understanding. One teacher that we interviewed had this to say about her students' metacognitive abilities: "Sixth grade students are starting to make connections and see how they relate to the whole. I guess that this is really the first time that they have this global view of it all."

An essential component of student choice in assessment is what Stiggens describes as the *growth portfolio* (cited in Willis 1997). Growth portfolios contain items that represent evidence of students' increased proficiency in specific areas of the curriculum. Students, for instance, may keep copies of their creative writing papers completed throughout the year, or collect mathematics assignments or projects that demonstrate integration of specific topics or principles they have studied. Students are given the opportunity to examine their own growth when they are held responsible for collecting and evaluating their school work. Personal attention to their progress can motivate students to improve performance and effort.

When we know the extent of young adolescents' cognitive abilities, we are dismayed with the overuse of traditional standardized assessment instruments such as multiple-choice tests. These instruments may have a negative influence on instructional decision making. They discourage teachers from using alternative instructional strategies that provide students with the time and opportunities to exercise their newfound cognitive abilities (Brown 1990).

Accepting Diverse Products

Teachers who use alternative assessment strategies provide options for students in developing individual plans for demonstrating their knowledge. Individualized assessment plans allow students to choose how they will demonstrate their learning so that assessment matches their abilities while building on their weaknesses. Teachers who adopt individualized assessment practices accept and account for differences among learners, whether created by culture, gender, developmental stages, or special learning needs.

One expectation of a meaningful assessment environment is that students demonstrate essential thinking processes in a variety of ways. Seasoned teachers understand that students develop competencies at varying levels and times. Saying that you recognize student differences is a beginning, but we have found that few teachers respond to these differences in how they assess students. Failure to adapt curricular and assessment decision making leads to teacher frustration and a likely decline in students' motivation as standards are established that some students are incapable of meeting. Establishing realistic individual outcomes for performance and learning results in more meaningful student learning and growth.

Authentic Assessment Leads to Meaningful Learning

Authentic assessment refers to genuine learning activities—opportunities students have to connect curricula to events occurring in their lives and to people with whom they interact. Authentic assessment emotionally engages students, as they use information in real-life contexts that have meaning to them (Schurr 1999). Tombari and Borich (1999) describe authentic assessment as "an outlook that says that the primary aim of testing is to inform and improve instructional decision making, rather than to label, grade, place, or select the learner" (5). Students engaged in authentic assessment activities develop plans to present information that they have learned to selected audiences—from peers to community members.

Examples of authentic assessment include student-generated activities such as developing oral presentations to explain research findings, constructing timelines, creating slide shows, writing song lyrics, creating maps, submitting a short story for publication in a local journal, or devising a research plan. These activities demonstrate how young adolescents are able to use many of their developing cognitive skills such as creative thinking and problem solving, rather than merely memorizing isolated facts, as is the case with many standardized and teacher-designed assessments.

Perhaps the greatest advantage of authentic assessment over traditional testing is the chance it provides young adolescents to extend their knowledge through reflection and application of information to real-life contexts. Authentic assessment is a dynamic process that cannot be confined to a forty-two-minute period one day a week.

Schurr (1999) summarizes the main components of authentic assessment. It:

- involves an audience or the public
- is not constrained by arbitrary or unrealistic time limits
- requires collaboration with others
- employs higher-level critical and creative thinking
- is complex, open-ended, and draws on many capacities
- uses students' own research or background knowledge as a means not an end. (3)

Of primary importance in using authentic assessment is that young adolescents need to be challenged in a way that encourages them to find solutions to personally developed questions and hypotheses. Students are motivated when they are engaged in these activities because they are the creators of their own learning—not recipients of a contrived curriculum evaluated by externally devised tests.

Performance Assessment

Many of you have designed, implemented, or participated in performance activities that may have also been assessments. These include athletic events, musical contests, dance recitals, driving tests, and submission of letters to the editor. Some common classroom performances include story writing, designing science laboratory experiences, and engaging in debates. Students participating in performance assessments demonstrate deep understanding of a topic through engaging in personally meaningful learning activities.

Students engaged in performance assessments must learn processing strategies and content knowledge simultaneously. In designing a visitors' guide to encourage people who visit a state, for example, students must utilize many cognitive processes: research skills to locate information, critical thinking abilities in choosing pertinent facts to include, creative thinking in designing the layout of the guide, and metacognitive strategies in designing rubrics to evaluate their final product. Many teachers have identified these processes—research skills, critical thinking, creative thinking, and metacognition—as the strategies that students must gain as a result of schooling.

Teachers should identify the specific process skills that they want their students to acquire as they develop student assessment practices in order to more effectively connect the processes and the products of assessment. That's the value of performance assessment—it encourages students to engage in specific processing strategies to reach the desired end result.

Effectively designed assessment practices, such as performance assessments, become the uniting force for content and process. An advantage of student-directed assessment is that it provides the learner with the opportunities to make these connections more meaningfully than he or she would with teacher-designed or externally-administered tests. Teachers are responsible for monitoring students' efforts while they develop their end products. Extensive teacher feedback ensures that students are acquiring necessary strategies and accurate beliefs about new principles and concepts.

Rubrics

One effective means of assuring that students' progress meets realistic, quality expectations is the development of rubrics to evaluate performance and products. Rubrics are scoring guidelines that provide a scale and a set of descriptors for varying levels of performance (Lewin and Shoemaker 1998). Figure 7.1 and 7.2 show two sample rubrics, one for assessing a persuasive essay and one for evaluating posters demonstrating students' understanding of bird adaptations.

The use of rubrics encourages students to become more reflective about their work. Rubrics can be used as guidelines if students are given access to them *before* they begin their projects. Rubrics are much more

4

Essay is well constructed as the author communicates the intended message clearly to the reader. Arguments are logically sequenced and respond to the issue being addressed. Each argument is well supported by research statements. Voice is appropriate for the nature of the topic being discussed. Author has effectively used appropriate conventions for formal writing. Creative solutions have been included that are realistic and apply to the problem being addressed.

3

Essay is reasonably well constructed. Arguments are supported by findings but not logically sequenced. Some sentences stray from the issue being debated. A few grammatical and spelling mistakes exist. Response shows minimum creativeness.

2

Essay contains a few effective components. Construction shows questionable organizational structure as supporting sentences are clearly written but out of place. Several spelling and grammatical mistakes exist, creating a text that is difficult to read. Response appears to contain some copied information with a lack of creative ideas for resolving the problem.

1

Essay is inadequate for the assigned purpose. Sentences address the problem but do not support the arguments presented. Text does not flow as sentences are unrelated to each other. Many spelling and grammatical errors make the text difficult to read.

Figure 7.1   Sample Rubric for Persuasive Essay Writing

4

All illustrations are accurate in their representation of the changes that birds have experienced. Evolutionary changes are labeled accurately. Changes that have occurred with at least five birds are shown on the poster. At least three separate adaptations are demonstrated. The distinctive markings used to identify the birds are drawn accurately.

3

Most of the illustrations are accurate in their representation of the changes birds have experienced. Four of the five evolutionary changes are accurately labeled. At least four birds that have experienced evolutionary change are shown on the poster. At least two adaptations are demonstrated. Most of the markings used are accurate representations of the birds.

2

Only two of the illustrations are accurate in their representation of changes. Three evolutionary changes are labeled accurately. Only three birds are shown on the poster. Only one adaptation is demonstrated. Most of the distinctive markings are inaccurate.

1

Most of the drawings are inaccurate representations of the changes that have occurred. Only one evolutionary change is labeled accurately. One or two birds are drawn on the poster. Explanations of adaptations are not clear. No distinctive markings are shown.

Figure 7.2 Sample Rubric for Evaluating Posters on Adaptation of Birds

descriptive than letter grades or percentage scores because they provide students with the specific feedback needed to improve on past performances and redirect their efforts as they work toward a finished product. These descriptors encourage growth instead of mere evaluation, as is the case with many traditional assessment instruments. Rubrics can be designed for any assessment task, and are most effective when developed in collaboration with students.

Portfolio Assessment

Portfolios are another potentially meaningful assessment tool for young adolescents. Schurr (1999) describes portfolios as a "systematic, integrated, and meaningful collection of a student's day-to-day work showing that student's efforts, progress, or achievement in one or more subjects" (4). Students are the primary decision-makers regarding which items to include in the portfolio and are also responsible for evaluating its contents (Schurr). Teachers, parents, and peers might also have a voice in deciding what to place in the portfolio. No mandates should govern portfolio creation; however, below are some examples of items that may be included in portfolios:

- student-established goals
- journal entries
- pertinent questions
- written hypotheses
- book reviews
- creative writing and graphic designs
- peer reviews
- video-taped presentations
- parents' comments on work
- teachers' comments
- self-evaluations
- self-designed rubrics
- evidence of collaboration with other students
- computer-generated projects

These are only a few suggestions for what you and your students may choose to place in a portfolio. Certainly the list and variety of items is endless. What is important is that the items represent the essential strategies and knowledge the student uses to explore significant themes.

The use of student-developed rubrics or checklists to guide decision making is helpful in encouraging students to engage in personal reflection of their progress in achieving personal academic goals. These checklists may provide students with guidelines for how to construct, design, and decide what may go into their portfolio. Student, peer, teacher, and parental written evaluations might also be included. Developing a student-oriented portfolio packet is an activity that promotes meaningful learning through engagement in the process.

Additional Assessment Strategies

Schurr (1999) uses the term *naturalistic observations* to describe how teachers determine a student's academic capabilities. She suggests that teachers "observe individual and group behaviors related to academic tasks, work habits, thinking processes, and other activities" (21). Some of you realize that your observations of students are the most reliable indicators of what a student can do in learning environments. This personal knowledge is necessary for assuring that students are challenged and succeed regularly in academic endeavors. Keeping an individual folder for each student provides teachers, parents, and the student with an opportunity to see development throughout the year. These folders may also serve as portfolios for some students.

Teachers who use performance and portfolio assessment are encouraged to involve students in their conferences with parents. Student-involved conferences put young adolescents in a position of authority over their academic growth (Willis 1997). Students involved in these joint conferences join their parents and teacher to discuss their progress throughout an academic term. Responsibility for clarifying what was learned and demonstrating knowledge acquisition lies with the student. Students have the opportunity to provide insights about their progress toward personally established outcomes. They share with their parents strengths and areas of needed growth as they display samples of their work. These conferences are empowering for students as the audience for their growth is more personally focused on them than in traditional teacher-led conferences.

Tombari and Borich (1999) refer to assessment techniques that educate the learner and the teacher as *growth-referenced assessment*. Teachers who adopt this view of assessing students most likely believe that "learning problems are caused by misconceptions or inadequacies in how learners think about or represent problems, not by inadequate abilities or prerequisite skills" (39). The emphasis in growth-referenced assessment is on using the data collected about a students' performance to find strategies to improve their learning opportunities. Few assessment strategies have this individualized goal in mind—a disturbing fact, considering that individual student growth is the primary goal of all instruction.

Support for Alternative Assessment

As you read this chapter, you may have experienced the excitement of discovering new strategies for determining what students are learning. Remember that assessment does not stand apart from curricular and instructional decisions. The integration of these three components must be accomplished if meaningful learning is to be achieved. The adoption and use of alternative assessments can be challenging, despite your newfound faith in employing these innovative strategies. Your colleagues can have a powerful influence on how you choose to assess students. Your principal can be influential in providing the support needed to use these strategies. Our encouragement alone may not be sufficient in influencing your assessment practice. As you read Chapters 8 and 9, think about the support systems you will need to initiate instructional models that assure genuine student engagement and learning.

References

BROWN, D. F. 1990. "The Effects of State Mandated Testing on Elementary Classroom Instruction." Ed. D. diss., University of Tennessee.

EDUCATORS IN CONNECTICUT'S POMPERAUG REGIONAL SCHOOL DISTRICT 15. 1996. *A Teacher's Guide to Performance-based Learning and Assessment.* Alexandria, VA: Association for Supervision and Curriculum Development.

LEWIN, L., AND B. J. SHOEMAKER. 1998. *Great Performances Creating Classroom-based Assessment Tasks.* Alexandria, VA: Association for Supervision and Curriculum Development.

SCHURR, S. 1999. *Authentic Assessment: Using Product, Performance, and Portfolio Measures From A to Z.* Columbus, OH: National Middle School Association.

TOMBARI, M., AND G. BORICH. 1999. *Authentic Assessment in the Classroom: Applications and Practice.* Upper Saddle River, NJ: Merrill.

WILLIS, S., ed. 1997. "Student-Involved Conferences." *Education Update* 39, no. 8: 1, 6. Alexandria, VA: Association for Supervision and Curriculum Development.

EIGHT

Altering School Structures

In the ideal middle school, we'd have soda and snack machines. You could have your choice of lunches instead of horse meat. Classes could be twenty-five minutes long. We'd have a free class where you could do whatever you want as long as you get your work done. Classes wouldn't be as boring. We'd have no lectures, and we'd have recess after lunch.

JUSTIN, EIGHTH GRADER

Responding to the needs of the young adolescent requires that we face the challenging tasks of reevaluating current curriculum models and instructional strategies. In Chapter 5 we suggested that the most appropriate model for middle school curriculum design is one that focuses on the questions and concerns that students have about themselves and their world. In this model, students collaborate with teachers in developing themes for study and are the driving force in developing ways to best explore those themes. They make decisions about what and how information should be studied. In Chapter 6 we focused on instructional strategies that put students at the center of classroom activities with the emphasis on learning, not teaching.

Implementing a curriculum design that focuses on student concerns and values student-centered instruction necessitates making changes in the structure and organization of the school day. Early adolescents' needs for movement and socialization, as well as their desires to be known and valued, also have implications for how staff, time, space, and resources are utilized.

In this chapter we ask you to examine a number of structures that have been implemented in exemplary middle schools to respond to student needs. Such structures include teaming, advisory sessions, and flexible scheduling.

Teaming—The Heart and Soul of the Middle School Concept

Teaming is often considered the most vital aspect of the middle school structural design and an identifying feature of true middle schools. The need for alternate educational structures was identified more than thirty years ago when William Alexander, a prominent figure in the early middle school movement, called for "a fundamentally different kind of organization utilizing team teaching and some aspects of a nongraded structure to provide a much richer experience for all the children" (Alexander 1998, 26).

The use of teaming has increased dramatically in the past thirty years, most significantly after the publication of the Carnegie Council's recommendations in *Turning Points* (1989). From the council's first recommendation—"School should be a place where close, trusting relationships with adults and peers create a climate for personal growth and intellectual development" (37)—came two specific suggestions that advocate the use of teams to transform middle level education.

> First, the enormous middle grade school must be restructured in a more human scale. The student should, upon entering middle grade school, join a small community in which people—students and adults—get to know each other well to create a climate for intellectual development. Students should feel that they are part of a community of shared educational purpose.

Second, the discontinuity in expectations and practices among teachers, the lack of integration of subject matter, and the instability of peer groups must be reduced. Every student must be able to rely on a small, caring group of adults who work closely with each other to provide coordinated, meaningful, and challenging educational experiences. In turn, teachers must have the opportunity to get to know every one of their students well enough to understand and teach them as individuals. Every student must have the opportunity to know a variety of peers, some of them well. (37)

The Carnegie Council specifically recommended that middle schools change by "creating smaller learning environments, forming teachers and students into teams and assigning an adult advisor to each student" (37).

The rationale for the development of teams focused on the problems inherent in the traditional structure of middle level schools—a departmentalized system based on the factory model (see Chapter 3). When students change classes every forty-two minutes for six to eight periods a day and are continually confronted with a new teacher and a new group of students, the close relationships that are so important for the young adolescent are more difficult to develop. The departmentalized, separate subject model also provides little opportunity for students to make sense out of the curricular material or to integrate knowledge across subject boundaries.

The team solution organizes teachers and students into small groups. The most predominant structure consists of four teachers from the four major content areas (math, science, language arts, and social studies) who have shared responsibility for 100 to 125 students and are empowered to make decisions about what is best for these students. The students move from teacher to teacher with the same group of peers throughout the school day.

In many middle schools, the team teachers continue to serve as subject specialists. Much of their curricular decision making throughout the school year reflects the dictated state or local mandates for their areas of expertise. Often, however, teachers are able to correlate topics so that ideas studied in one subject area complement what goes on in another area. An example of such "parallel" teaching, as described in Chapter 5, is the study of the Revolutionary War in history class correlated with the reading of *Johnny Tremain* in language arts.

Well-functioning teams and teams that have common planning times have the opportunity to move beyond the departmentalized approach and engage in collaborative planning. Teachers may develop multidisciplinary thematic units that involve all teachers on the team. These themes are chosen by teachers and each teacher determines how his or her subject area can contribute to the study of that topic.

The most powerful use of the teaming concept, however, is in the context of the curriculum integration model (see Chapter 5), when themes are chosen and units developed collaboratively with students. The boundaries between subject areas dissolve, and team teachers ask not how their subject area expertise can contribute to the theme topic but how they can best facilitate student learning. Collaborative planning with students would be virtually impossible to implement in a traditional setting.

Some middle schools use two-teacher teams comprised of a small number of students. Others add a fifth member to four-person teams, such as a reading teacher or special subject instructor (e.g., music, art, physical education). In some schools, multigrade teams are developed with seventh and eighth grades on the same team and often in the same classes. Team structures can be as varied as the students they serve. Decisions about teaming should be made after considering space, time, staffing, and student demographic issues.

Less than 10 percent of middle schools in the late 1960s were using a team structure (McEwin 1997). This amount had increased by the late 1980s to about 33 percent and by 1993 more than 59 percent of middle schools were using this approach. Still, despite teaming, "in the majority of all middle level schools, departmentalization continues to dominate—isolating teachers, fragmenting curriculum and letting thousands of young adolescents 'fall through the cracks'" (McEwin, 322).

Benefits of Teaming

Benefits to Students

> The best thing about school is that in some ways I like the teams. I know my teachers and like being with other grades. The teachers get close to you.
>
> MEG, EIGHTH GRADER

In order to be an effective organizational scheme, teaming must produce a learning environment that meets the needs of middle level students. Can teaming, when implemented correctly, support the young adolescent's growth toward independence by providing a means to enhance cognitive growth, nurture emotional growth, enable social growth, and recognize the realities of physical growth?

Curriculum and instruction are most definitely enhanced by the effective use of interdisciplinary teams. We have already discussed how thematic teaching helps students make connections across subject areas, thus avoiding the fragmentation that is often experienced in a departmentalized structure. Learning can be integrated throughout the school day with each teacher providing specific content and skills to help students explore significant themes. In addition, collaboration with students increases motivation and enthusiasm for learning.

When teams have some control over the class schedule, students have the opportunity to explore ideas for longer periods of time. Flexibility in teaming allows for time to engage in the in-depth research, analysis, and project development that is difficult using a traditional approach.

Teaming helps nurture emotional growth in two ways. First, the team approach helps students cultivate closer relationships with teachers and with each other. Students begin to develop a sense of belonging and community that enhances their own personal identity. Students know that there is always an adult they can turn to for assistance. Second, teachers develop a better understanding of student needs. Teachers are able to discuss individual student concerns at team meetings, analyze problems, and develop solutions to better meet the needs of each child. In departmentalized middle schools, collaborating with colleagues about student needs is difficult due to time restrictions and isolation of both teachers and students.

When students spend the entire day with a single group of peers, they have more of an opportunity to develop close relationships with them. Teachers can involve students in cooperative activities and encourage social interactions. Peer relationships are thereby improved.

Teachers who have control over the scheduling of classes and instructional strategies are better able to respond to the physical needs of young adolescents. When students are in forty-two-minute-long classes, teachers often feel pressure to meet curricular deadlines. They may feel that they don't have time to either allow students the freedom of movement they need or to discuss young adolescent health and personal concerns that are often central to students. Teaming allows more time for varied instructional strategies that focus on active learning, not only enhancing cognitive growth but responding to students' physical needs.

Benefits to Teachers
While the benefits of teaming to students are clear in terms of both cognitive growth and school climate, teachers also reap rewards from this structure. Research has indicated that teachers involved in teaming perceived that they participated more, had more opportunities for decision making, and experienced more cooperation than teachers in traditional departmentalized settings (Walsh and Shay 1993). Teachers also believed that they were more supportive of students and more receptive to their needs and ideas. In contrast to teachers in traditional settings, teachers involved in teaming saw their students as more motivated and involved.

Certainly teachers in schools that support a team concept experience less isolation than teachers in departmentalized schools. They can collaborate on instructional issues as well as share their concerns about students. As teachers become empowered to make increased decisions about what's best for their students, morale is improved and a sense of increased professionalism permeates the school.

Instruction also becomes more effective. Teaming allows for diversity in teaching styles, flexibility in scheduling, and expansion of professional input. Improved relationships with students and parents are also apparent.

Drawbacks to Teaming

I don't have any idea why they have us on teams.

ROB, EIGHTH GRADER

In a perfect world, with a perfect school run by perfect administrators filled with perfect teachers, we would see perfect teams. These teams would be empowered by the administration to make curricular, instructional, and scheduling decisions for their students based on a shared vision of the purpose of education and their role as educators. They would have a common planning time in which decisions could be made and concerns discussed. Teachers would develop their strengths and rely on other teachers to support and nurture them.

But it's not a perfect world. As with any organizational structure, the promise of the team's benefits is at times overshadowed by the reality of its implementation. In the world that we live in, personalities clash, philosophical differences exist, teachers feel threatened, and planning time is limited. Some of the difficulties in teaming are the result of whole-school policies. Adequate planning time depends on the availability of shared space and time. Effective administrators can help you solve some of those problems.

The more difficult considerations are the problems that arise because of teachers' personalities, insecurities, inflexibilities, and fears. When a teacher becomes certified, that does not automatically assure that he or she knows how to work with other professionals on a team. The most effective teams have had to work very hard to get where they are. Tuckman (1965) describes four levels of team development. A good professional development program in a school can enhance and assure the success of most teams as they work their way through these stages.

In stage one—*forming*—the team of teachers experiences the excitement of starting out on a venture that they believe will benefit students. The team seeks a purpose and a vision and works to build community.

Relationships are not always easily formed, hence the next step—*storming*. This stage arises as different personalities and differing philosophies about curriculum, instruction, discipline, and student expectations come into play among the members of the team. Poor communication skills may contribute to conflict. Teachers question their values and procedures and must learn how to meld personalities and differences into a system that works.

With good facilitation, during the next stage—*norming*—teachers can develop a clearer vision of the team goals and the role of each member in achieving those goals. Teachers begin to feel confident in their strengths while recognizing the strengths of the other teachers on the team. On the flip side, they become willing to acknowledge their weaknesses and learn how to accept the weakness of other team members. Ideally, they begin to see how their strengths and weaknesses can complement those of the other team members. Roles are defined, and trust between team members is achieved.

The team is then ready to act—this is the *performing* stage. Planning begins and choices are made. Members are committed to the vision of the team. In forming teams, teachers must learn to focus on students. It's a challenge replete with pitfalls. But as Erb (1997) comments, "Teams where teachers engage in dialogue about matters of mutual concern do reflect new levels of teacher interaction leading to the creation of novel solutions to educational problems" (39).

Although teaming has the potential to enhance socialization some students feel that it actually impedes their social interactions. Sheila (seventh grade) didn't like the team concept at her school. "I don't get to see my friends very often. We're all mixed up on weird teams with eighth graders. Half of my friends are all the way across the school, and we only get to see each other during extra-help period. One of my best friends from last year I never get to see." LeAnne, a seventh grader at a different school, agrees. "I have to stay with the same seventy people all day long. I never get to see the people I got close to last year."

Another potential problem facing the use of teams relates to those students with special needs or diverse learning styles. Not all teachers work equally well with all students. When teams have the maximum flexibility to determine curriculum and scheduling, students have the minimum flexibility to be with teachers who might better meet their needs. Should we, in fact, be placing students on teams regardless of their specific learning needs or should we be choosing the teachers that will best respond to their needs? One eighth grader with special learning needs commented, "I don't like teaming. I have ADHD. My science teacher is okay, but I don't really get along with the rest of my teachers. I know there are probably other teachers in the school that would understand me better but they won't let me off team."

Incorporating the contribution of teachers of special subjects such as music, art, physical education, computer technology, and foreign languages presents another challenge to teaming. Teams do not usually include teachers of these subjects because grade level teachers are best able to meet together when all of their students are attending classes with the music, art, or physical education teachers. But again, the importance of an exploratory curriculum in which students are exposed to new ideas cannot be overlooked at the middle level. Not including special-area teachers on the teams once again fragments student learning and may give the message to students that those classes are less important. Administrators must work to ensure that special-area teachers are a vital part of the overall planning process for students.

Frequently teams exist in name only. Although teachers may share students and at times are able to meet to discuss their concerns about them, middle level educators often remain subject bound, engrossed in their own area of expertise without regard to what the rest of the team is doing. If teaming is simply an organizational structure, the full benefits of this construct will not be obtained. If students are still sent through the day as in the factory model, traveling from class to class on a rigid forty-two-minute schedule, with no integration throughout the school day, faculty may as well revert to the departmentalized model. In the best of worlds, "Teams provide friendship in a hostile world, a point of reference in the endless cycle of schools. Perhaps this is why interdisciplinary teaming has become the key to the most effective middle schools" (Golner and Powell 1992, 32).

Developing Advisory Programs

> The quality of the relationship between teachers and students is the single most important aspect of middle level education.
>
> VAN HOOSE (1991, 7)

> In our advisory, the topics we discussed were peer pressure, safety, how to stay away from drugs, and how to bring our careers together.
>
> MICHAEL, EIGHTH GRADER

When we look at the multitude of issues facing young adolescents, it is amazing that anyone gets through middle school without incurring some type of permanent emotional distress. On a daily basis, young adolescents face:

- dealing with physical changes
- making new friends
- being a member of the "right" peer group
- developing independence from parents
- avoiding peer pressure
- going steady with boyfriends/girlfriends then breaking up
- finding a sexual, cultural, or ethnic identity
- being harassed by other students
- handling the pressures of academic demands.

To assist students with the many social and emotional pressures that they face through the middle level years, some middle schools are developing advisory programs. NMSA identified advisor/advisee programs as an essential element of effective middle school design (NMSA 1995). In addition, as you recall, the Carnegie Council focused on the need for teachers to develop close relationships with their students (1989). Specifically, they stated that "Every student needs at least one thoughtful adult who has the time and takes the trouble to talk with the student about academic matters, personal problems, and the importance of performing well in middle grade school" (37).

Despite these endorsements, few middle schools have adopted advisory programs. Several reports during the 1990s revealed that less than half of middle schools surveyed had developed advisory programs (Galassi, Gulledge, and Cox 1998a). George and Oldaker (1985), on the other hand, reported that 93 percent of middle schools identified as exemplary used advisory programs.

In an advisory program, an advisor (usually a teacher) meets with a small group of students on a regular basis for the primary purpose of helping students develop trusting relationships with an adult and close social bonds with a small group of classmates. Advisory sessions may be designed for student-to-student and student-to-teacher discussions about personal topics related to young adolescence. These sessions are essentially nonacademic, ungraded, and planned with young adolescents' social and emotional interests and needs in mind.

Advisory sessions can be designed in any number of flexible time arrangements to meet the scheduling demands of each school. For instance, some schools have advisory sessions that meet once a week for thirty to forty-five minutes; other schools schedule advisory twice a week; alternately, advisory may take place every day for fifteen to thirty minutes. A study by McEwin, Dickinson, and Jenkins (1996) revealed that in schools with advisory programs, most met daily, with the most common length being from sixteen to thirty minutes.

The time at which advisory sessions are offered and the length of the sessions may have an impact on the effectiveness of the programs in meeting students' needs. Advisories scheduled for the end of the school day may be perceived as of low priority. Short time periods (less than fifteen minutes) may not provide adequate opportunity for students and teachers to engage in conversations that address students' social and emotional needs.

Students can be grouped with grade-level peers during advisory sessions. Some schools have multiage advisory sessions in which sixth, seventh, and eighth graders are grouped heterogeneously. The developmental differences among young adolescents at each grade level may lead to the belief that separating students by grade level would best meet the needs of the students. Data collected from middle level students in one study, however, indicated that the majority of students surveyed preferred cross-grade advisory groups (Ziegler and Mulhall 1994). An advantage of cross-grade advisory groups is the opportunity for younger students to become acquainted with and receive support and advice from the older students in the building.

In some schools, students remain with the same advisor and advisory group for their entire middle school career, providing increased opportunities for students and advisors to become well acquainted. Gill and Read (1990) reported that fifteen nationally recognized experts in middle level education suggested that students remain with their advisors for all of their middle level years. Students surveyed in one study indicated, however, their preference for changing advisors each year (Sardo-Brown and Shetlar 1994). Not surprisingly, students prefer to choose their own advisor and undoubtedly would like to have the opportunity to switch to a different advisor if they feel the need.

It is primarily teachers who serve as advisors, but to reduce the ratio of advisees to advisors other professionals in the building, including counselors, administrators, librarians, and district specialists, are often assigned a group of advisees as well. Becoming a proficient advisor requires initial training and regular attention to the specifics of how to organize and deliver an effective program to students. Advisors must be willing to develop a relationship with students different from the one they experience as a regular classroom teacher—one characterized by caring, not authoritarianism (Cole 1992). James (1986) suggested that many students view their "advisor as more of a friend or advocate than a teacher" (53). The expectations for teachers to develop caring and trusting relationships with students and to be willing to discuss personal thoughts and feelings during advisory are frequent obstacles to obtaining teacher support for an advisory program (Galassi, Gulledge, and Cox 1998b). Some teachers are not comfortable with or accustomed to becoming socially and emotionally involved with their students. These teachers will struggle as advisors if not properly trained prior to the initiation of an advisory program.

Why Young Adolescents Need Advisory Programs

> I like advisory because the whole class is my friends and those are the people I met first. You have the same advisory for all three years. Not all advisories are good but mine is. The teacher helps me a lot. Once I was really upset, and he could tell, and he really helped me with my problems.
>
> CELESTE, EIGHTH GRADER

> Those who know this process say with certainty that an advisory system makes a school a more personal place; gives all advisors a chance to share something powerful; provides students and parents a specific person in the school to whom they can turn with questions, concerns, or offers of help; and has a generally salutary effect on the overall culture of a school.
>
> GOLDBERG (1998, 63)

Advisory programs can support students' growth toward developing a positive identity. Many of the questions and concerns that students have could be addressed through a curriculum designed by students as described in Chapter 5. Their questions, however, may not generally elicit a response from teachers in regular classrooms where academics commonly receive much greater emphasis than social or emotional concerns.

The heart of a successful advisory program is the development of a trustful, caring community in which students perceive their advisor as demonstrating unconditional support for their growth. Galassi et al. (1998b) describe the type of relationship that should exist between students and teachers: "Middle school advisory programs provide an opportunity for both advisors and advisees to belong to a 'family,' a chance to secure physical and emotional affiliation" (9). Elizabeth, a sixth grade teacher in a wealthy school district, provided this thought: "Because parents are so busy at their jobs, the children are neglected. Someone's not there to listen to them—or for them. Their friends here at school become their family." An urban middle school teacher, Denise, explained her strategy for developing trusting relationships: "I develop trust by treating students like they were my own children—I will tell them I love them. I think kids can pick up quickly how much you care or don't care."

Advisory groups also respond to young adolescent needs for positive social interactions. A seventh grade teacher, Pamela, describes some social issues that create a need for advisory sessions: "I think grades are important to these students, but I think their number-one thing is friends, and that's their biggest fear: not having the right friends, not having certain friends, and being accepted." Advisory sessions provide students with a base, if you will—a place that they can call their home away from home.

Advisory groups also provide young adolescents with the opportunity to discuss issues and questions about their personal lives—particularly health and sex related issues. When asked about her advisory sessions an eighth grade student, Karen, from an urban school district, said, "I'd like to talk about sex education, cause most kids when they're at home with their parents don't talk to them about what happens during puberty." We expect middle students' questions about such personal issues to be answered by an adult. If parents aren't comfortable speaking about these sensitive topics to their children or if their children won't allow them to, then teachers must take the responsibility for doing so.

Recent gun violence at middle and high schools is evidence of the great need for emotional support that an advisory group can provide. Cole (1992) suggested, "When a crisis hits a school, such as the death of a student or family member . . . the TA [Teacher Advisory] group may become literally a life saver as all students have an immediate way of talking about the incident in a place where they already belong, with an adult whom they trust" (32). Advisory groups can provide more than a safe haven in a crisis. The presence of an advisory program can, in fact, help to stem such violence. We will see violence decrease when all children feel a part of a group and feel valued and wanted.

Choosing an Appropriate Focus

A major objective of many advisory programs is the development of meaningful relationships between students and teachers. Advisory programs, however, may be designed for other reasons. John Galassi, Suzanne Gulledge, and Nancy Cox in their NMSA publication titled *Advisory Definitions Descriptions Decisions Directions* (1998b), describe possible emphases for advisory programs:

1. *advocacy emphasis*—focuses on addressing students' individual needs and personal concerns in the development of close relationships between the student and teacher in delivering a developmental guidance program
2. *community focus*—emphasis is on addressing students' social needs; providing a feeling of belonging for students as advisory groups develop a family atmosphere
3. *skills program*—focuses on helping students to develop skills in the areas of understanding self and others, problem solving, decision making, academic success, community involvement, and career awareness
4. *invigoration type*—an activity emphasis where students and teachers engage in fun activities to reduce the stress associated with academics with offerings such as intramurals, club activities or service projects
5. *academic advisory*—promotes academic growth through activities such as sustained silent reading or the introduction of study skills
6. *administrative emphasis*—much like a homeroom situation where students are given information or money is collected for lunch or field trips—mainly involves housekeeping tasks

The program developed at each middle school may have one of these foci as its primary objective or a faculty may decide to combine several of these or other objectives throughout the year. Cole (1992) suggested a daily advisory session with a different focus each day. For example:

156

Monday—relationship building activity
Tuesday—intramurals
Wednesday—silent reading
Thursday—relationship building activity
Friday—tutorial or independent study. (10)

Reviews of the literature on studies of advisory programs indicate that "students prefer activities that are fun, less structured, stimulating, relevant to their own lives, and over which they can exercise some degree of choice" regardless of the focus of advisory (Galassi et al. 1998b, 51). Bushnell and George (1993) discovered that males and females had a different set of criteria for judging the effectiveness of their advisors: females wanted advisors who showed they cared and wanted to talk; males were interested in advisors who showed respect for their opinions and joked around.

Many practical details must be resolved before an advisory program can be implemented. Cole (1992) suggested that the following issues be addressed:

- Who [will] serve as an advisor?
- What training do advisors get?
- When and how often do advisories meet?
- Which students are assigned to which advisors?
- What resources are available for the advisory program? (12–13)

In addition, the focus of the advisory program must be determined. Teachers and administrators should collaborate with students to develop the most effective program for their school. When teachers unilaterally make decisions about how the advisory program is structured, student needs may not be addressed. One sixth grade student, Peter, commented, "I think advisory groups are pointless because you don't really do anything. We play silent ball—just throw a ball around and if you drop it you're out. We just play stupid games and do stupid papers. It would be worthwhile if we did something in it but we don't."

Implementation of an advisory program can be quite challenging. Some parents, teachers, administrators, and students may be heavily opposed to adding a nonacademic program to the school's schedule. Teachers may be especially concerned that they are not trained in counseling techniques. In addition, some teachers feel that their job is primarily academic, and they should not be required to help students with challenging emotional issues or other personal concerns. These are valid responses. Despite the problems involved in developing an advisory program, such a structure can play a vital role in helping students through the social and emotional challenges they experience during their young adolescent years. Many sensitive issues are on students' minds, and by ignoring these issues, teachers may prevent classrooms from becoming true learning environments.

Studies that provide direct evidence to support the effectiveness of advisory programs in altering student behavior and improving middle school environments are few; however, those studies that have been conducted report favorable views on the value of advisory programs (Galassi et al. 1998b). We believe that a program that can provide student support through this challenging stage of development should be implemented in middle level schools for the sake of young adolescents.

Flexible Scheduling

> A key feature of the transformed middle grade school should be flexibility in the duration of classes. Teacher teams should be able to change class schedules whenever, in their collective professional judgment, the need exists. They should be able to create blocks of time for instruction that best meets the needs and interests of the students, responds to curriculum priorities, and capitalizes on learning opportunities such as current events.
>
> CARNEGIE COUNCIL (1989, 52)

According to the NMSA Research Summary on Flexible Scheduling (1999), the primary organizational structure for the middle schools is still the factory model in which students attend seven or eight forty-two-minute classes throughout the day. The bell announces when students move on to the next class and they must get there in three or four minutes. Teachers provide information and little time exists for in-depth study, research, or analysis.

Such an organizational structure results in numerous difficulties. According to Canady and Rettig (1995), one of the greatest problems of a traditional schedule is the effect on a school's climate. Many of the discipline problems that occur in school happen during the time that students are changing classes. With a traditional schedule, you may have 1,000 students in the hall at the same time six or seven times a day.

Another difficulty with traditional scheduling is that it does not provide students an opportunity to become deeply involved in their studies or to see connections in their learning. Because the school day is broken up into small segments, students can't do extended research or get involved in major projects. In their look at innovative scheduling, Canady and Rettig maintain, "Students traveling through a six-, seven-, or eight-period day encounter the same number of pieces of unconnected curriculum each day, with little opportunity for in-depth study" (5). Some students require more time to learn. This time is not available in the traditional schedule.

One solution to the above problems is the development of a flexible schedule—one that optimizes learning experiences for the students. Time then becomes a positive resource rather than a barrier to student learning. Teachers are not bound to the clock and the bell, but are free to make professional decisions regarding the best ways to meet the needs of students.

Chuck, a seventh grade social studies teacher, saw a positive change in the school climate when his school instituted flexible scheduling. "From a discipline standpoint, block scheduling is definitely affecting kids in a positive way. When teachers spend less time on classroom management, there's more instruction happening."

Dan, an eighth grade social studies teacher, has seen the impact of flexible schedule in the achievement of his students: "I cover 25 to 30 percent less content today than I used to; but, I teach it better, and the kids understand it better." Jim, who teaches mathematics in seventh grade, agrees, "I think more information is sticking with these students with eighty-minute periods. They have opportunities to think about why they are performing certain functions and operations. I find most of my former students are doing better in eighth grade after they've had the block."

Ronald Williamson (1998), in his book *Scheduling Middle Level Schools: Tools for Improved Student Achievement*, supports the idea that the traditional six or seven learning periods a day, in addition to inhibiting teachers' creativity, constrains learning and does not respond to the developmental needs of the young adolescent. He says, "Examining and refining the structure of the school day—the use of time—has a profound impact on the school's ability to provide for the learning needs of its students" (8–9). The schedule should be a tool controlled by student needs rather than the bell. We need to look at alternative ways to structure learning experiences. Maybe all classes don't need to meet every day. Maybe every subject doesn't need to meet for the same amount of time. Maybe students don't have to have the same number of classes every day.

Types of Flexible Scheduling

Flexible scheduling is just what it says it is—flexible. A number of models have been implemented. Successful middle schools adopt models that best meet the needs of their students—accommodating changes as needed.

Block Schedules

In the block approach, the schedule is designed around blocks of time, usually eighty to ninety minutes. These expanded periods of time provide teachers with the opportunity to engage students in interdisciplinary studies. In addition, students have the time to become involved in in-depth projects and research.

Block scheduling allows and demands that teachers use diverse instructional strategies. Certainly if students are in the same class for longer periods, traditional instruction will not work. Chuck, a seventh grade social studies teacher commented on how block scheduling has changed the way he teaches. "The block scheduling has forced me to be more diverse in my teaching. I tended to be more teacher centered—

now, I'm more child-centered. . . . I have absolutely changed instruction. I use much more hands-on strategies now, such as Internet activities, projects, research in the library, a lot more in-depth discussion, and a lot more critical thinking."

If teachers do not change instructional patterns, the use of block scheduling could be a disaster. Jesse, an eighth grader, didn't like the use of block scheduling in his school. "I don't like classes that are one and a half hours long. It's kind of stupid to have it that long. They should be like forty-five minutes." Jesse is an adolescent with attention deficit hyperactivity disorder (ADHD). Unless instruction is active and varied, the long block would be very difficult for him.

Block scheduling is not without its difficulties. Schedules must be developed around special classes such as music, art, and other exploratory courses. Teachers must change their teaching patterns, and common planning time for teams becomes an imperative.

Rotating Schedules

Although block scheduling provides extended periods of time for study and projects, other forms of scheduling have also provided flexibility in meeting student needs. With a rotating schedule, students meet classes at different times each day. On Monday, students might have one class that meets for the first two periods of the day. On Tuesday, they have advisory the first period and the block meets the second and third periods—blocks in the morning and afternoon might shift. Some students may learn best in the morning, others after lunch. Some teachers do their best teaching in the morning, others after lunch. A rotating schedule gives all teachers and students the opportunity to interact with each other at some time during their optimal learning times.

Dropped Schedules

With dropped schedules, not every class meets each day. This option allows for schools to add advisory periods, exploratory classes, and other special units. In addition, it provides teachers with the flexibility of staying with a group for an entire day to complete projects, and then meeting with another group the next day.

No best model for flexible scheduling exists. Each model has its advantages and disadvantages as well as the logistical difficulties inherent in any schedule. How do we schedule lunch, languages, music, art, technology, and other special subjects while still providing a schedule that is responsive to the needs of the young adolescent? Teams of teachers and administrators must work with students to find the model that works best.

The NMSA reports that only about 20 percent of middle schools implement flexible scheduling of some kind (1999). When looking at exemplary middle schools, however, researchers indicate that approximately 75 percent of those surveyed use some type of flexible scheduling. Middle level teachers must begin to focus on maximizing learning opportunities for students. That may mean replacing traditional views of how the school day is structured.

Concluding Reflections

Making a difference in the lives of young adolescents requires that we reform and transform middle level education. In addition to curriculum, instruction, and assessment that validate students' questions and concerns, changes in the school structure can help create more powerful learning environments. Meeting the needs of middle level learners is a challenging and exciting task. We have the opportunity, through listening to students, to make school a place that makes sense to young adolescents and helps them find meaning in their lives. The final chapter of this book encourages you to become an advocate for young adolescents, supporting those programs that enhance their growth and developing new programs to meet their needs.

References

ALEXANDER, W. M. 1998. "Program and Organization of a Five through Eight Middle School." In *Moving Forward From the Past: Early Writings and Current Reflections of Middle School Founders.* ed. R. David. Columbus,

OH: National Middle School Association and Pennsylvania Middle School Association, 14–26.

BUSHNELL, D., AND P. S. GEORGE. 1993. "Five Crucial Characteristics: Middle School Teachers as Effective Advisors." *Schools in the Middle: Theory into Practice* 3, no. 1, 10–16.

CANADY, R. L., AND M. D. RETTIG. 1995. "The Power of Innovation Scheduling." *Educational Leadership* 53, no. 3: 4–10.

CARNEGIE COUNCIL FOR ADOLESCENT DEVELOPMENT. 1989. *Turning Points: Preparing American Youth for the 21st Century.* New York: Carnegie Corporation.

COLE, C. 1992. *Nurturing a Teacher Advisory Program.* Columbus, OH: National Middle School Association.

ERB, T. O. 1997. "Thirty Years of Attempting to Fathom Teaming: Battling Potholes and Hairpin Curves Along the Way." In *We Gain More Than We Give: Teaming in Middle Schools*, eds. T. S. Dickinson and T. O. Erb. Columbus, OH: National Middle School Association, 19–59.

FORBES, E. 1944. *Johnny Tremain.* Boston: Houghton Mifflin.

GALASSI, J. P., S. A. GULLEDGE, AND N. D. COX. 1998a. "Middle School Advisories: Retrospect and Prospect." *Review of Educational Research* 67, no. 3: 301–338.

———. 1998b. *Advisory Definitions Descriptions Decisions Directions.* Columbus, OH: National Middle School Association.

GEORGE, P. S., AND L. L. OLDAKER. 1985. *Evidence for the Middle School.* Columbus, OH: National Middle School Association.

GILL, J., AND J. E. READ. 1990. "The 'Experts' Comment on Adviser-Advisee Programs." *Middle School Journal* 21, no. 5: 31–33.

GOLDBERG, M. F. 1998. *How to Design an Advisory System for a Secondary School.* Alexandria, VA: Association for Supervision and Curriculum Development.

GOLNER, S. J., AND J. H. POWELL. 1992. "Ready for Teaming? Ten Questions to Ask Before You Jump In." *Middle School Journal* 24, no. 1: 28–32.

JAMES, M. 1986. *Adviser-Advisee Programs: Why, What and How.* Columbus, OH: National Middle School Association.

McEwin, C. K. 1997. "Trends in Establishing Interdisciplinary Team Organization in Middle Schools. In *We Gain More Than We Give: Teaming in Middle Schools*, eds. T. S. Dickinson and T. O. Erb. Columbus, OH: National Middle School Association, 313–324.

McEwin, C. K., T. S. Dickinson, and D. M. Jenkins. 1996. *America's Middle Schools: Practice and Progress—A 25 year Perspective*. Columbus, OH: National Middle School Association.

National Middle School Association. 1995. *This We Believe: Developmentally Responsive Middle Level Schools*. Columbus, OH: National Middle School Association.

National Middle School Association. 1999. "NMSA Research Summary #2: Flexible Scheduling." National Middle School Association. www.nmsa.org.

Sardo-Brown, D., and J. Shetlar. 1994. "Listening to Students and Teachers to Revise a Rural Advisory Program. *Middle School Journal* 26, no. 1: 23–25.

Tuckman, B. W. 1965. "Developmental Sequences in Small Groups." *Psychological Bulletin* 63: 384–399.

Van Hoose, J. 1991. "The Ultimate Goal: AA Across the Day." *Midpoints* 2, no. 1: 1–7.

Walsh, K. J., and M. J. Shay. 1993. "In Support of Interdisciplinary Teaming: The Climate Factor." *Middle School Journal* 24, no. 4: 56–60.

Williamson, R. D. 1998. *Scheduling Middle Level Schools: Tools for Improved Student Achievement*. Reston, VA: National Association of Secondary School Principals.

Ziegler, S., and L. Mulhall. 1994. "Establishing and Evaluating a Successful Advisory Program in a Middle School." *Middle School Journal* 25, no. 4: 42–46.

NINE

Being an Advocate
for Young Adolescents

*Adolescence is one of the most fascinating and complex
transitions in the life span: a time of accelerated growth and
change second only to infancy; a time of expanding
horizons, self-discovery, and emerging independence; a time
of metamorphosis from childhood to adulthood. Its beginning
is associated with profound biological, physical, behavioral,
and social transformations that roughly correspond with the
move to middle school or junior high school. The events of
this crucially formative phase can shape an individual's
entire life course and thus the future of our society.*

THE CARNEGIE COUNCIL (1996, 7)

By now you are convinced that young adolescents need a distinctive learning environment to serve their particular needs, that they
deserve an exciting, meaningful learning experience, and that being a middle school
teacher is the right job for you—or not.

In the first chapter of this book we asked
you to list the characteristics you felt a middle
school teacher needed to have. Have your
ideas changed? We heard what middle level
students told us. "They should be nice." "They
should make learning fun and interesting."

"They should care about us." Listen to middle level students. Listen intently to what they have to say to you. Sit at the lunch table with them. Chat with them in detention and as they wait outside the principal's office. Listen to students as they roam through the halls or respond to other teachers. Volunteer to chaperone a middle school dance. Observe band and choral rehearsals. Attend track and soccer practices. Eavesdrop on the conversations that occur during physical education classes or at the bus lines after school each day.

Young adolescents are vibrant, alive, curious, energetic, and exciting to be around. They need a school environment that responds to these qualities. Too often their schools are dull, detached, and sometimes even cruel places. These students are captives of a system that suppresses their natural needs, capacities, and desires.

What do young adolescents need?

- curriculum that is relevant and meaningful
- instruction that is challenging and active
- assessment that responds to diverse intelligences and learning styles
- kind, caring teachers who listen to students
- adults who know them well and whom they can trust
- opportunities to socialize with peers
- a healthy and safe school environment

Young adolescents are changing dramatically and those changes demand that we create a suitable learning environment. As young adolescents make that often frightening move from the dependence of childhood to the independence of adulthood, teachers need to support them, to enjoy them, and to provide guidance as they search to make meaning out of the many changes occurring in their lives.

Support for Middle Level Reforms

A comprehensive look at research on middle level reform (Lipsitz 1997) includes the report "The Impact of School Reform for the Middle Years" (Felner et al. 1997). The authors presented results from a longitudinal study that analyzed the degree to which each of the Carnegie Council recommendations in *Turning Points* (1989) had been implemented in specific schools and the resultant impact on student achievement and behavior. The researchers divided the schools into those with the highest levels of implementation of the Carnegie recommendations (including common planning time for teachers, a small number of students on teams, the presence of advisories, changes in the teaching-learning process, and curriculum reform), those at medium levels of implementation, and those with no implementation. A diverse mix of schools were represented at each level. In the seven years in which data were collected, ninety-seven schools were studied.

The results of the analysis indicated significant academic gains and personal growth when the Carnegie Council recommendations were implemented. Students from those schools reflecting high implementation scored consistently higher than state norms in mathematics and language and reading assessments. Students' scores from schools with the lowest levels of implementation tended to be at or below state averages.

Similar patterns were found in terms of student behaviors. Teachers from the more fully implemented schools reported far lower levels of student behavioral problems including aggression, learning difficulties, and emotional distress. On self-reports, students from the more implemented schools showed less fear, depression, and anxiety and had higher levels of self-esteem. As the authors indicated, "Clearly, across quite different types of sources of data (e.g., achievement tests, teachers' reports, student self-reports), there are distinct differences between schools that have attained different levels of implementation of the *Turning Points* recommendations" (Felner et al. 1997, 545).

Middle school faculty who implement only portions of the Carnegie recommendations are not realizing the full impact that total implementation can have on middle level students. Too often faculty and administrators change the school structure without changing instructional and curricular practices. Many middle level faculty place students on teams, however, the teachers are given little if any common planning time and limited decision-making authority over the schedule or the curriculum. With no opportunities to collaborate on curriculum, no control over instructional issues, and little opportunity to discuss individual learning needs, young adolescents are denied optimal growth opportunities. Authors of the Felner et al. (1997) report found the following problems associated with inadequate implementation of the *Turning Points* recommendations:

- Teams fail to engage in critical teaming activities that focus on curriculum integration, coordination, and collaboration around student needs/assignments.
- Students report a more negative school climate.
- Students and teachers report increased psychological and behavioral problems.
- Student achievement lags. (548)

The authors concluded, "It appears that when schools attempt to implement these practices but do them poorly (e.g., one or two common planning times per week, interdisciplinary instruction without common planning time, large teams), there may be no effect or even negative effects, especially on teacher attitudes and student performance" (548).

Teachers and administrators must pay more than lip service to the implementation of recommendations for middle level reform. Lipsitz (1997) reported that "reforms implemented independently of one another are likely to produce little or no significant rise in student achievement, especially for disadvantaged youth. Not until a critical mass of reforms is in place and operating together in an integrated manner do significant positive changes in student outcomes occur" (519). Faculty that change school structure but not curriculum or instruction may be seeing positive changes in school climate, but they will not experience the maximum benefits of students' academic growth until the integration of curriculum, instruction, and assessment becomes the focus of change.

Supporting Young Adolescents

What do these research findings mean for you? You must speak out. Do not be content with being a teacher in a middle school in name only. As middle level educators, we have a responsibility to be advocates for those programs that improve the quality of education for young adolescents. Clearly the data show that gains in achievement as well as improved student behavior and emotional adjustment are the result of implementation of recommendations for middle level reform. These gains are representative for all including at-risk students. If we implement reforms that group students to ensure success, provide a common core of knowledge for all, expand opportunities for learning, maximize the use of time and space, and involve students in decision making with respect to their learning, many of the needs of the young adolescent will be addressed.

Not only must we develop a community of learning in middle level schools, we must also garner parental support and community resources. We have discussed at length the pressures that exist against many middle level reform policies, including societal expectations, legislative dictates, parental fears, mandated tests, and concerns about high school or college entrance. Joining professional organizations, attending conferences, and reading professional journals are all vehicles that can enable you to expand your knowledge base and keep current on middle level reform. You must then share this knowledge with administrators, parents, and other adults so that we can continue to help young adolescents grow.

The *True* Middle School

A primary objective in writing this book was to describe the characteristics and conditions needed to create a true middle school. Some of you will say that creating such a school is not possible or practical. We know it is possible because year after year more teachers and administrators are establishing a vision, developing a plan, and implementing the components that we have described in this book. They establish teams, collaborate with students on curriculum and instruction, institute flexible schedules, and, in effect, create successful middle schools.

The critical components needed to establish effective middle schools don't spring from politicians' mandates, administrators' policies, school board members' proposals, or parents' complaints. They develop when teachers speak clearly, loudly, and with knowledge about what is best for young adolescents, and then act on those pronouncements.

A true middle school reflects much more than program or structural reforms, however. It is more than just a place of learning. It is a place where students experience the support of caring adults who provide liberal amounts of prodding, encouragement, understanding, and celebration to the experiences that young adolescents encounter. A true middle school is a place where students are genuinely valued—not merely in words but in the very way that they are treated.

We've asked many middle school students what advice they would give to someone who wants to be a middle level teacher. Their suggestions are straightforward and from the heart.

> "My advice to people wanting to be middle school teachers is to be strong. The students are going to give you a hard time. You need a lot of patience and you have to make it fun. Being in middle school is really hard."
>
> "My advice to teachers is to listen to the kids' half of the story, get to know the kids, get to be their friends and not just a teacher—but don't be too much of a friend."
>
> "Be nice."
>
> "My advice to teachers is that when you're telling someone what to do, don't yell. Be more open minded. Don't think, 'My way or no way.'"
>
> "Teachers need to be more understanding or they won't last."
>
> "Be humorous. Do not be mean to the kids. Don't be strict or very demanding."
>
> "I think anyone who wants to be a teacher better check to make sure they have a sense of humor. It is important to be funny sometimes when dealing with kids."

You either already are or want to be a middle school teacher. You want to make a difference in the lives of young adolescents. Right now you are on top of the mountain. If you feel that you have what it takes to work with young adolescents, to validate them and encourage them and help them learn, push your poles into the ground and go. It will be an exhilarating ride. You will surely fall. But you will also fly.

References

CARNEGIE COUNCIL ON ADOLESCENT DEVELOPMENT. 1989. *Turning Points: Preparing American Youth for the 21st Century.* New York: Carnegie Corporation.

CARNEGIE COUNCIL ON ADOLESCENT DEVELOPMENT. 1996. *Great Transitions: Preparing Adolescents for a New Century.* Abridged Version. New York: Carnegie Corporation of New York.

FELNER, R. D., A. W. JACKSON, D. KASAK, P. MULHALL, S. BRAND, AND N. FLOWERS. 1997. "The Impact of School Reform for the Middle Years." *Phi Delta Kappa*, 78, no. 7: 528–532, 541–550.

LIPSITZ, J., A. W. JACKSON, AND L. M. AUSTIN. 1997. "What Works in Middle-Grades School Reform." *Phi Delta Kappan* 78, no. 7: 517–519.

Index